PRACTICE AND POLITICS

an Essential Reader
for Social Workers *and* Therapists

edited by Rahim Thawer, MSW, RSW

THE POLITICIZED PRACTITIONER™ SERIES, VOLUME 1

Blue Cactus Press | caləɫali

ʔukʼʷədiid čəɬ ʔuhigʷəd txʷəl tiiɬ ʔa čəɬ ʔal tə swatxʷixʷtxʷəd ʔə tiiɬ puyaləpabš. ʔa ti dxʷʔa ti swatxʷixʷtxʷəd ʔə tiiɬ puyaləpabš ʔəsɬaɬaɬlil tulʼal tudiʔ tuhaʔkʷ. didiʔɬ ʔa həlgʷəʔ ʔal ti sləχil. dxʷəsɬaɬlils həlgʷəʔ gʷəl ƛ̓uyayus həlgʷəʔ gʷəl ƛ̓uƛ̓axʷad həlgʷəʔ tiiɬ bədədəʔs gʷəl tix̌dxʷ həlgʷəʔ tiiɬ ʔiišəds həlgʷəʔ gʷəl ƛ̓uʔalalus həlgʷəʔ gʷəl ƛ̓utxʷəlšucidəb. xʷəla···b ʔə tiiɬ tuyəlʼyəlabs.

Blue Cactus Press is located in caləɬali, on puyaləpabš land. This land was stolen and colonized by settlers via the signing of the Treaty of Medicine Creek in 1854. Since then, it has not been returned to its rightful and traditional stewards, puyaləpabš, also known as the Puyallup Tribe of Indians.

We acknowledge that we benefit from our existence at caləɬali. We are thankful to live, work, and be in relationship with the land and people here.

For Zachary—gone but not forgotten. You helped me appreciate the rainy days.

Table of Contents

Foreword

PRATYUSHA TUMMALA-NARRA, PH.D.

Therapists today are grappling with a legacy of neglect and minimization of social context and oppression in clinical theory and practice. The contemporary global context, which is rife with structural and interpersonal marginalization, calls for innovations in how we think about human development, psychopathology, and psychotherapy. Too often, in the quest for new theories and practices that reckon with social injustice, there is a tendency to devalue existing mainstream perspectives. This volume, *Practice and Politics*, challenges the social, cultural, and political bases for established clinical theories with nuance, rather than diminishing their value in understanding unconscious and conscious dimensions of a person's life. Rahim Thawer has brought together an excellent group of contributors who explore the distinct ways in which social, cultural, and political contexts shape human suffering, identity, relationships, healing, and empowerment.

Reflective of the social work tradition that pioneered a contextual focus in mental health, the authors in this volume center intersectionality and fluidity of the self as empowering experiences rather than deficits. They caution us about the problem of pathologizing cultural experiences and norms, such as those concerning immigration, gender, sexuality, social class, neurodiversity, and body image. Drawing on various theories, such as psychoanalytic, Gestalt, and decolonial frameworks, they highlight the role of unconscious and conscious processes that shape the psyche and relational life, and their impact on anti-oppression work. They take up difficult affective experiences (e.g., anger, grief, guilt, shame, and envy) as essential components of anti-oppression, healing, and the therapeutic process. Notably, they walk the reader through their own journeys with marginalization and anti-oppression work in their personal lives, training, practice, and research.

It is rare to see such a volume that places at the foreground the therapist's social and political identities, social locations, and perspectives, in addition to the therapist's own experience of marginalization and privilege. As Thawer notes, therapeutic work is inherently political, characterized by a dynamic exchange of implicit and explicit communication regarding the therapist's and the client's life experiences, attitudes, and biases. Tensions can and do emerge, as the therapist and client determine what can and cannot be said and what can and cannot be repaired in their relationship. The wide range of case illustrations in this volume offer an opportunity to delve into what these tensions concerning social context, suffering, oppression, and empowerment feel like and how a therapist may engage with rupture and repair with a client. The authors courageously share their countertransference in challenging therapeutic moments and how they used their reactions to guide precarious conversations with their clients, which are critical for growth. Relatedly, they point out both the importance of self-reflection and the complex binds that emerge around self-disclosure.

One of the most poignant contributions of the volume is the authors' powerful, strength-based structural analysis of trauma and violence. They rightfully challenge individualistic interpretations of trauma which have become commonplace in popular global culture, like those evident in the notion of "narcissistic abuse," which dismisses the structural problems that perpetuate violence. The authors aptly observe how easily we can make the fallacy of diverting structural and political causes of human suffering into the confines of personality traits of perpetrators or deficits within survivors.

This volume challenges traditional approaches to psychotherapy and quantitative research as the gold standard. For example, the reader is invited to consider how psychoanalytic theory can inform community-based interventions, such as counseling sessions implemented in a bathhouse to help men who are navigating connection alongside risk related to HIV and other sexually transmitted infections. The authors further invite us to expand our understanding of reflexivity in research, including how we interpret data based on our own social locations and experiences. By doing so, they highlight dilemmas concerning what evidence constitutes in mental health research, practice, and training.

In each chapter, readers will find themselves questioning what underlies long-standing and well-established theories and practices and re-envisioning how we think about the interaction of the psychic and the social. As someone who has been working toward centering sociocultural context within psychoanalytic theory, and more broadly theories of development and psychopathology, this volume brings me substantial hope as it offers a new generation of promising advances in clinical theory that center sociopolitical realities.

Practice & Politics

On Being a Politicized Practitioner

RAHIM THAWER, MSW, RSW

Agree or disagree: If a client brings up something political, it's our job not to engage.

This is one of many questions I've posed to social workers, counselling students, and psychotherapists in my workshops across Canada and South Africa. People have strong feelings about politics and whether or not they belong in the clinical space. Some suggest it's our role to be engaged in current political discourse and prepared to engage with the topics brought forth by our clients. Others argue that we have to work hard to maintain and "hold space" until there's an opening to explore the personal impact and emotional consequence of what's being shared. Relational therapists, whether Gestalt or psychoanalytic, would infer that the client brought this topic up because of the very people that are in the therapeutic relationship — that it's part of the 'relational field' or the transference — and therefore cannot be seen as merely incidental to treatment.

I invite you to read the remaining multiple-choice questions from my workshop surveys and consider how you might respond. Reflect on whether or not your position on each question has evolved since your initial clinical training.

How do you understand the value of 'self-determination' in social work or psychology?

    a) Professional

    b) Political

    c) Both

How do you understand the value of 'sex-positivity' in direct practice?

    a) Professional

    b) Political

    c) Both

How do you understand the value of being 'pro-choice' in direct practice?

    a) Professional

    b) Political

    c) Both

If I'm working at a community organization that serves people living in poverty, my work is:

    a) Professional

    b) Political

    c) Both

If I'm working at a community organization to support people living with HIV, my work is:

    a) Professional

    b) Political

    c) Both

There's a new addition to your outreach or clinical team. Your co-worker says to you that she only got hired because she's a woman of color. You are likely to:

a) Say nothing

b) Agree with the co-worker

c) Challenge the statement

You're in a consultation meeting and a colleague says, "I have an attention-seeking female client that wants to use male pronouns." You are likely to:

a) Say nothing

b) Agree with the co-worker

c) Challenge the statement

If a client brings up something political, it's our job not to engage.

a) Agree

b) Disagree

c) It depends

If a client were to say, "It's hard for me to find work because there are too many immigrants willing to work for less," I believe:

a) This is within my scope to address/explore

b) I'm comfortable responding

c) I'm uncomfortable responding

d) I would feel triggered

If a client says, "I feel like I'm treated differently at work as a Black person," I believe:

   a) This is within my scope to address/explore

   b) I'm comfortable responding

   c) I'm uncomfortable responding

   d) I would feel triggered

A client says, "My eldest child is having difficulty. Her teacher thinks the cause is ADHD, and they want to put her on medication. I'm worried." I believe:

   a) This is within my scope to address

   b) I'm comfortable responding

   c) I'm uncomfortable responding

   d) I would feel triggered

Overall, I believe my professional work is political.

   a) Agree

   b) Disagree

   c) Unsure

Reflect on your responses overall. Is your work ethic more or less political than you might have initially thought? What are the nuances that came up when you considered your responses to these questions?

Our clinical approach and appreciation of the scope of practice will inevitably be informed by our own social locations: age, race, gender, disability, sexual orientation, and class. As a result, different emotions and intensities will be evoked in the therapist based on their own lived experience and political orientations. For example, when I circulated this survey, almost all respondents indicated they were comfortable with responding to the concerned mother whose child is being evaluated for ADHD. However, when it comes to a client's subjective experience of racial mistreatment, respondents indicated a range of responses, among them a feeling of being personally triggered. When the racialized therapist is triggered in this context, it can lead to a range of trauma responses: over-identification in a fight response, redirection in a flight response, or dissociation in a freeze response. Most survey respondents shared in the discussion that they wanted to believe the client at face value. Others stated the importance of maintaining some level of curiosity about the context and where the experience fits into individual behavioral patterns. This approach is absolutely okay (you're not inherently 'blaming the victim' by being curious). However, curiosity without the politicized lens about how racism operates, and more specifically how anti-Black racism operates, can instead be experienced as persecutory suspicion that works against the client's interest.

Developing a politicized lens with clients at the center

People want to talk about political events in therapy because they are directly affected by them in their daily lives. Climate crises, the cost of living, bodily autonomy, police brutality, and fears of being stripped of constitutional rights are but a few of many politicized issues that may arise. My social work training lends itself to an entry point that utilizes anti-oppression as a framework for interpreting these large-scale topics. Anti-oppressive perspectives dominate the political left so clients who are culturally saturated in these narratives will need their therapists to help them separate a structural analysis from interpersonal dynamics, microaggressions from narcissistic injury, and historical marginalization from residual anger.

As therapists, we listen on multiple levels. In my own practice, I listen with a political ear, a psycho-dynamic ear, and a cognitive-behavioral ear, but also a Gestalt heart. These ways of listening are what distinguish therapy from mere conversation. As a politicized practitioner, I notice that it's harder for me to access my own empathy when a client seems to have a strong perspective that's working against them. For example, I've had numerous clients bring to therapy their charged positions on inter-community conflict, like publicly exposing a person who has caused harm (sometimes overstated as abuse), actively engaging in an internet war (phone in hand, Twitter feed open) during a session, or choose to call the police on a neighbor in a community where the police likely aren't well equipped to respond appropriately.

I can recall the tightness in my chest when a gay male client processed in therapy whether or not he would want to report HIV non-disclosure from one of his sexual partners (who posed little risk for actual transmission to my client). Politically, I am firmly against the criminalization of HIV non-disclosure. However, I needed a way to access my empathy so I could also listen on other levels. I affirmed that summoning the state to intervene in his relationship was an option but that I'd like to explore other parts of his experience. I asked about when my client's anger actually began for the man he'd been pursuing. We identified that the problem was actually about the other man's emotional unavailability which felt cold before they even had sex. It turned out, this also mirrored the kind of coldness he experienced from his family of origin, particularly his father and older brother. This meant that the man he'd been pursuing for some time was triggering past interpersonal trauma and leaving him anxious about the possibility of rejection or mistreatment. With this in mind, we considered if calling the police was actually about accountability from the sexual partner (again, who posed no risk to the client) or displaced anger about long-standing mistreatment from the men in his life.

Moments like these challenge therapists to suspend their strong reactions and create a safe container for the issues that invite anger and distress. While a therapist can never truly be a blank slate, the effort to maintain some neutrality and grasp for curiosity in place of a punitive response is important (and specifically our job). A therapist sharing too much of their own political analysis (too quickly, without exploratory questions) is poorly managing their own countertransference. This response is a disservice to the client and the profession.

When it comes to politically-based countertransference, Spangler, P. T. et al. (2017) wrote,

> We as psychotherapists are as subject to the political climate as any member of society. In managing any countertransference, gaining awareness is the first step, specifically by recognizing our political hot button topics and the triggers for them. Are there particular topics that rile? Does denial of global warming or scientific methods in general set you off? Or are questions about voter fraud likely to be a focus of unresolved material? Whatever the issue, awareness that it is a trigger is important, as is understanding the underlying source of the countertransference.

Consider a South Asian woman in her late 30s whose family migrated from India to Canada in the 1970s. She comes to therapy to talk about her anger toward her mother for being oddly competitive and mildly narcissistic. Her therapist, also a South Asian woman, deploys her political analysis inappropriately by (unintentionally) siding with the mother and introducing the impact of migration and racism on the nuclear family. The client can access this kind of affirmation and systemic analysis through community care. She needs her therapist to cultivate cultural safety by being aware of the trauma of immigration while also holding space for the anger toward the 'bad mother.' Being a politicized therapist isn't about proving to your client that you have a particular systemic analysis; rather, it's about understanding the political context and intervening in a way that is meaningful for your client as an individual.

In cases where clients are immersed in the realm of the political, our task is often to hold space for the deep impact of both proximal and distal events, support psychological integration of the material (i.e. facilitating somatic and cognitive metabolizing), nurture safety so that grief can be identified and expressed, and help our clients access a clearer mind as they proceed. Our interventions are individual and therefore limited. We know from our clinical experience, however, that individuals who feel supported by their therapists can participate more optimally in collective settings.

Vignettes, deconstructed

Conservative psychiatrist Dr. Sally Satel argues that anti-racism and critical race theory are "encroaching" on a profession that should be neutral and apolitical. I disagree with her wholeheartedly. However, I do believe the following statement by Satel (2017) to also be true:

> When therapists use patients as receptacles for their worldview, patients are not led to introspection, nor are they emboldened to experiment with new attitudes, perspectives, and actions. Patients labelled by their therapists as oppressors can feel alienated and confused; those branded as oppressed learn to see themselves as feeble victims."

Nevertheless, I also cannot imagine a clinical assessment that is not grounded in a political context. Below I have provided a snapshot of four different clients I have worked with, followed by notes on what a purely medical model and apolitical way forward might be. I then offer notes on the political context from my worldview and discuss my politically informed clinical approach with each client.

Client A

Snapshot:
Client A misuses her morphine prescription but also feels that her disabilities and perpetuated poverty leave her with little joy in her life.

She has a visual disability and had chronic pain issues at a young age that eventually required her to use a wheelchair long-term. As with most people who experience chronic pain over a long period, her tolerance for medication has increased over time. She routinely 'runs out' of pain medication and is unable to get a prescription refill from her doctor.

Medical, apolitical approach:
Client A needs substance use counselling combined with CBT for depression; perhaps budgeting support.

Political context:
Client A's poverty and pain are very real. An initial desire to focus on behavioural health discounts the systems that keep her poor (she receives less in social assistance monthly than what most people received for CERB — Canada Emergency Response Benefit: biweekly financial support for employed and self-employed Canadians who were directly affected by COVID-19). This focus would also make me, as a professional, morally superior. When she drops out of therapy, I can easily conclude that she wasn't ready for change. So, is the misuse of the morphine a problem? Partially. But if I can't get her affordable housing or strong-arm the city's mayor to start caring about disabled people, my politically-informed approach is to ensure she has a dignified space to explore her trauma with an understanding that her current problem isn't with addiction; it's with limited resources.

My approach:
I explored the client's relationship to morphine. We talked about what it allows her to feel temporarily and what emotional pain it enables her to escape. We gently acknowledged that morphine is soothing physical and emotional pain. I empathized with her shame for being labelled as "drug seeking" while also recognizing that she probably can't be prescribed more. I recall saying, "I understand this drug is your friend, she (the medication) is very dependable, but I want for you to be able to make it last to the end of the month so that you're able to get a dose

of the warm feels on some of the harder days." She agreed that this was reasonable as long as she could vent from time to time about how the system holds her back. "Of course!" I said.

Client B

Snapshot:
Client B experiences very real microaggressions as a queer Black man. He has a complex trauma history, including incestual abuse. He has borderline personality disorder. He endorsed this diagnosis but doesn't like the stigma that comes with it. Client B is acutely aware that such a diagnostic label might lead others to minimize his experiences. His day-to-day concerns were about alcohol dependency, emotional dysregulation and underlying contempt in numerous interactions.

Medical, apolitical approach:
BPD requires skills training in dialectic behaviour therapy, substance use counselling, and anti-psychotic medication to help manage paranoid patterns of thinking (particularly when client drinks too much).

Political context:
As a Black man, he's part of a population that tends to be over-diagnosed with mental illness. He's smart and knows this. I want him to know that I know, too. Alcohol is a socially sanctioned substance and we are all (myself included) trying to consider what moderation looks like. Alcohol likely supports emotional regulation and facilitates access to emotion but works against him when there's too much anger that comes to the surface. Psychotic symptoms (e.g. paranoid delusions) should be treated, but they are also an amplified form of anxiety; that anxiety is embodied and tells a story.

My approach:
I began where he was at talking about race and racism. He was diagnosed by a white psychiatrist and lamented, "What if this diagnosis

was designed to make the psychiatrist feel more powerful or perhaps to keep me from progressing in life?" We created space to both grieve that this has been true for many, but likely not in his case. We identified the hostility that gets activated in the power dynamic with his psychiatrist. Underneath, he longed to become a psychiatrist and work specifically in his own community to protect his people from harm.

We explored the BPD diagnosis at length: "What does this label mean to you and how do you understand it? What do you think it summarizes about your past? What does it mean for you in everyday interaction? In what way do the criteria of this diagnosis make you feel relieved and/or defensive?"

Then we addressed the function of alcohol and underlying anxiety. I worked to hold space for his paranoid thinking and the shame underpinning his narcissistic injuries, while also helping him see the evidence of his own skills, talents and positive attributes that comprise his self-worth. We agreed there are times when he experiences anxiety more intensely or feels slights from other people more deeply than others might — that's the BPD at work. I didn't dispute that microaggressions exist in his world (because I believe they do), but we talked about how his reaction to them might be different given his baseline anxiety, frequent state of inebriation and early experiences of trauma. The politicized goal for therapy was not skills-based training (though I did refer him out to attend a group); rather it was to neutralize the stigmas of his diagnoses, unearth the schemas following his sexual abuse, and as the therapist, offer "the gleam of the mother's eye" (Kohut, 1971) that was never afforded to him as a child.

Client Q

Snapshot:
Client Q lost his friend to a drug overdose one year ago. He is having trouble finding work and getting out of bed. He's recently moved

back in with his family of origin due to financial constraints. He is also working to manage his symptoms of bipolar disorder and prevent relapse with opiate use.

Medical, apolitical approach:

The client may benefit from grief counselling, structured relapse prevention and CBT to disrupt the onset of manic or depressive episodes.

Political context:

If we pay attention to harm reduction activists, they would first reframe the problem: the client's friend died from lack of a safe supply, not an overdose. The lack of safe supply is about drug policy; many substances are criminalized, drug testing kits are not widely available, and supervised consumption services are scarce. Deaths related to unsafe supply are largely ignored because drug users have been ejected from mainstream society — particularly if they are poor.

My approach:

I offered politically informed grief therapy. We created space for anger toward the system that let their friend die. We processed the ways in which their late friend was vilified postmortem and the ways people tended to individualize the problem of addiction. We established cultural safety by my willingness to talk about systemic oppression. This foundation allowed us to explore the concept of disenfranchised grief and the isolation that accompanies it. The therapeutic relationship then felt safe enough for the client to move through some of the stages of grief and to express anger toward their late friend: "He should have quit using when I did…I should have intervened…he knew how to get his drugs tested, why didn't he?"

Client R

Snapshot:

Client R is a trans woman with a serious mental illness who is also seeking vaginoplasty surgery. When she's referred to me, her physician's goal is to help her contain her anxiety, auditory hallucinations (there's always a person upstairs keeping her awake on purpose), and persecutory delusions (there's a complex web of people and organizations working against her). The client wants to see me for a readiness assessment in order to pursue gender-affirming surgery.

Medical, apolitical approach:

This client, due to her state of mind and unwillingness to take psychiatric medication, cannot appreciate the risks related to surgery and therefore cannot provide informed consent. Further, any surgical complications may lead her to mistrust the surgeon making it difficult to provide any further care.

Political context:

This woman came to Canada as a refugee many years ago. In her country of origin, where she identified as a gay man, she feared for her life. She has a trauma history and, at present, her window of distress tolerance is minimal (meaning she's easily triggered and subsequently speaks in a louder, impassioned way that can seem confrontational). When people are afraid of her reactions, they likely cannot appreciate how transmisogyny and racialized sanism can operate at once.

My approach:

Most clients who are specifically seeking a readiness assessment spend two or three sessions with me before I can produce an adequate letter. Many more clients enter therapy wanting psychosocial support and merely identify pursuing surgery as a future goal. In this therapeutic relationship, the client and I spent 12 sessions together before a letter could be produced. She needed me to hear her experiences: her migration story, her traumatic experiences of persecution, and her frustration with the impact of being over-medicated on an inpatient unit many years ago.

I became a container for much of her dysregulation and anger. We slowly talked through the things her other providers couldn't: their concerns about liability, clarity about her surgical expectations, the prospect of future mistrust, the consequence of not following a post-surgical dilation regimen. She asked me if I believed that people were "against her." I said, "I have no doubt that you've been treated badly. I don't share the view that everyone is presently working against you. But it doesn't matter because you have a right to surgery." We also talked about the possibility that she will suspect her care team isn't working in her best interests. The alternative thought we landed on was this: "Providing me with good care is connected to their reputation so I should assume they want to do their best." My drive to support this client was nothing short of political.

Politically-informed clinical inquiry

In their article Navigating the Minefield of Politics in the Therapy Session, Spangler, P. T. et al. (2017) discuss the concept of political cultural competence, particularly following the 2016 American election of Donald Trump, which left the country divided: personal identities became about political affiliations. They state:

> "...few training programs address political affiliation as a component of culture or identity or how it may inform treatment or affect the therapy relationship. When clients bring differing political views into the therapy room, it can cause us unease, a sense of not knowing the way forward. It requires us to bracket our views and our privilege and dive beneath political opinions contrary to our own to

find the human being and the experiences at the source of these opinions."

Review the case studies below. Each is written with the reader as the therapist. The clients either bring up something specifically political or their statements require the therapist to be politically aware to some degree. I will provide some notes on the politicized layers of the case and then lead with a sample of exploratory questions that I hope will demonstrate political-cultural competence.

Case Study 1: Anil

This client is in his early 30s, racialized and heterosexual. He has been assigned to you for case management after being discharged from the hospital. He was admitted for severe alcohol dependency that led to psychotic symptoms and a suicide attempt. To begin to work with Anil, you come up with a safety plan and harm reduction strategies. At the end of your second meeting, he shared that he doesn't feel safe at home. When you probe further, he says that his neighbors are a gay couple, and he believes they embody the devil and are using black magic to disrupt his sobriety. As a social worker and a queer person, you feel activated by this.

Political and conceptual notes:

» Anil could be unaware that I'm queer and he's plainly homophobic.

» He could have a tacit awareness about my queerness as the therapist that makes him want to bring this up with me (which would be a relational interpretation).

» Facing addictive patterns brings out hopelessness in many people; a scapegoat narrative is common.

» Talk of magic and the supernatural is part of many cultures.

Clinical inquiry:

» You bring up something interesting that we haven't talked about. Can you tell me a bit about your spirituality and experience with magic?

» How do you make sense of your struggle with alcohol and recovery before you lived next door to this couple? What was driving it then?

» It seems a lot of emotion comes up for you when you talk about the neighbors. What upsets and intrigues you about them?

» I don't know that we can do anything about the neighbors unless you want to move. What are some additional factors, ones that we can control, that affect your alcohol dependency?

Case Study 2: Karena

Karena is 28, female, and white. She has been referred to you through an employee assistance program. Karena works at a finance company and has been having difficulty focusing. Recently, she made a series of small mistakes on an important client account and was reprimanded. She told her manager she was struggling. When you begin to work with her, you identify quickly that she is struggling with anxiety driven by self-doubt and an unsupportive partner. As you empathize with her and begin to explore the issue, she states that her Black co-workers are very loud and disruptive, which makes it hard for her to do her job. You're taken aback by this statement.

Political and conceptual notes:

» The client's narrative is clearly informed by anti-Black racism.

» Neurodivergence is often overlooked in women and plants the seeds for perfectionism, anxiety, and social challenges.

» Patriarchal gender socialization often allows men to be absent in relationships; in this case, it may have led the client to seek power and control in other ways.

Clinical inquiry:

» Can you share a bit about how you have fit into work and social situations throughout your life?

» What you describe sounds like it could be disruptive to your work, but the image that comes up in my mind is one of being left out. Is that part of why you feel upset with your colleagues?

» You've identified that negative self-talk or self-blame is primarily what holds you back. How long has this been true? Where do you suspect it originates?

» When you see other people getting along well and when you're not included, I wonder if it activates a kind of shame for you. Shame can make us feel inferior and lead us to bring others down. Could this be true in this scenario?

» Do you suspect there's a connection between race and conversational style? Were you aware that you were relying on a racial stereotype about Black women when you initially described the problem?

Case Study 3: Mubin

Mubin is a 38-year-old male, straight and single. This client self-refers to you for private therapy services (and you are a woman). He states that his last three relationships have failed and he is feeling very frustrated. The first three sessions are fairly calm and he participates willingly and fully. In session four, you begin talking about jealousy. You say that it's normal but can also be toxic. Mubin gets agitated and says, "You women always criticize men, but what about when you cheat on men and treat us like garbage? My ex basically forced me to stalk her." You take a pause and feel your heartbeat pick up pace.

Political and conceptual notes:

- » The transference of 'the dismissive partner' began when he selected you as a therapist; this attack is an important re-enactment (though it might feel a bit scary for the therapist).
- » Mubin may or may not be aware of his power and privilege in the world; he might have a men's rights movement mentality.
- » He's probably anxiously attached and asks for love/reassurance in a way that's too aggressive.
- » This client is in pain and desperate but is also a misogynist.

Clinical inquiry:

- » I'd like to slow us down. We began by talking about you, and then it was suddenly about all women versus all men. Have you felt embroiled in a gender war of sorts? Tell me about when or where that began.
- » When you spoke earlier, you said "You women." I wonder if you're afraid that you'll be vulnerable with me and then I'll treat you badly. How do you imagine that will play out?
- » Jealousy usually shows up when we feel threatened in some way. In your last relationship, what were you worried about? Were you worried that you would be replaced?
- » What would it mean or say about you if your partner wanted to be with someone else?

Conclusion

Clients will seek out therapists based on their political stripes, just as they do for preferences of gender, sexual orientation, and race. This is absolutely reasonable. However, the presumption of absolute value alignment is faulty. We cannot reduce people to their social locations of race, gender, class, sexual orientation, or disability. No one is just that one thing. But as therapists, we also have to be ready to engage with the politics of identity. Clients will inevitably bring politics into a session and we have to decide how to manage it. Being able to identify when you're feeling triggered or defensive in response to a client's statements is an important step toward successfully moving through the therapeutic process. Most of my therapy clients have scanned my social media profiles before contacting me. They know when to opt out. Someone who is staunchly Zionist likely won't want to work with an anti-apartheid therapist like myself. Having spent hours examining such a case in my own clinical supervision, I know that my counter-transference may render me a poor match for this type of client. But make no mistake — they also deserve mental health care. And, if they wanted to work with me it would be my responsibility to sort through the conscious and unconscious dynamics at play.

Social workers and therapists are doing political work on an individual level. Conceptualizing our practice as political doesn't mean we need to express political opinions. Rather, our politics get expressed in the way we do our work with clients (Sharma, 2019). Clients are presenting problems that often have political roots — we must be conscientious about when it's appropriate to explore the symptoms, the environment, or the political context.

The politicized practitioner is not morally superior or always right; rather, they are aware of their politically-based countertransference while trying to access their own empathy. They know when to seek supervision and they can appreciate that their worldview is constructed. As a politicized practitioner, I believe everyone deserves access to health care, which includes access to mental health services. In a world made up of oppressive systems, helping and healing are both inherently political.

References

Satel, S. (2021). When Therapists Become Activists. *American Enterprise Institute*, www. aei.org/op-eds/when-therapists-become-activists/

Spangler, P. T., Thompson, B. J., Vivino, B. L., & Wolf, J. A. (2017). Navigating the minefield of politics in the therapy session. *Psychotherapy Bulletin*, 52(4). Retrieved from https://societyforpsychotherapy.org/navigating-the-minefield-of-politics-in-the-therapy-session/

Sharma, P. (2019). Should therapy be political? Influence of social factors on mental health may make a case for such an approach. *Firstpost*. https://www.firstpost.com/living/should-therapy-be-political-influence-of-social-factors-on-mental-health-may-make-a-case-for-such-an-approach-6942831.html

Challenging Monogamy in Relational Sex Therapy: A Social Justice Approach

CARM DE SANTIS, MSC, RP, RCFT

My positionality

As a queer, multi-relational, cisgendered therapist, my professional approach is deeply informed by my lived experiences and commitment to social justice. My work is shaped by the intersection of personal identity and over 30 years of academic and clinical training, which challenges traditional, relational, and therapeutic norms.

My formal training began in a couple and family therapy program rooted in both traditional systemic therapies and postmodern approaches such as Dialogic, Solution-Focused, and Narrative therapies. This foundation, combined with over 500 hours of client work, 200 hours of supervision, and sex therapy training, deeply influenced my practice. While the program was groundbreaking in its focus on inclusivity and attention to power dynamics, it also revealed systemic limitations that continue to shape my understanding of social justice in therapy.

Currently, I am a practicing relational and certified sex therapist, registered psychotherapist, and clinical supervisor based in Ontario, Canada. My academic role includes teaching for over 20 years in the Department of Sexualities, Relationships, and Families Studies at St. Jerome's University. My doctoral research focuses on consensual non-monogamy, exploring the ways in which dominant monogamous paradigms influence relational and sex therapy.

Positioned within both the cultural and professional landscape, I now turn to the central issue at hand: the pervasive influence of monogamy in relational and sex therapy.

The Need for a Social Justice Approach in Therapy

The current monogamous framework in relational sex therapy reinforces societal power dynamics that marginalize non-normative relationship structures. By dismantling monogamy as the default, therapists can adopt inclusive practices that challenge systemic inequalities and align with social justice principles. Specifically, a social justice approach in therapy interrogates mono- and heteronormative discourse, which prioritizes heterosexual monogamy while relegating diverse relational structures to the margins.

A social justice approach in sex and relational therapy is not merely a method of client care—it is a sociopolitical stance. As a therapist, supervisor, and educator, I position myself as a politicized practitioner, engaging in activism both inside and outside therapeutic spaces. This activism involves critically examining and challenging entrenched norms of "coupledom," aiming to transform power dynamics at both interpersonal and systemic levels.

Critical thinking, as articulated by hooks (2010), is an active process of discernment and questioning—one that interrogates ideologies, practices, and methods. Within this context, challenging mono- and heteronormative discourse means unpacking dominant ideas about commitment, romance, love, and sex. It means asking who is permitted to engage in relationships and sexual connections, and why these permissions are structured as they are.

In practice, this involves disrupting and deconstructing the notion of monogamy as the aspirational relational structure within relational and sex therapy. By reframing these conversations through a social justice lens, this paper explores how therapeutic practices can move beyond the limitations of monogamous frameworks, fostering spaces for diverse relational structures to thrive.

Critique of Mononormativity in Therapy

Dismantling monogamy in relational and sex therapy research, training, and practice is my deliberate act toward social justice in this clinical and research field. The "dismantling" process requires taking apart a system and intentionally reducing or disrupting its power purpose. Monogamy is the mono- and heteronormative patriarchal apparatus of sanctioned relationships— it is the system I attempt to disrupt. This mono- and heteronormative apparatus is embedded in our Judeo-Christian patriarchal Western social structures and systems, which promote and uphold monogamy. Heterosexual coupling is rendered "ideal," "normal," and "superior" in a sexual, romantic, or intimate relational structure (Rubin, 1984; Schippers, 2016; Stelboum, 1999). This relegates other forms of meaningful connection and relational configuration as less undesirable, insignificant, and unrecognized. With a foundational understanding of social justice in therapy, it is essential to explore the historical critiques of monogamy, highlighting the voices and movements that have paved the way for current discussions."

Historical and Theoretical Context

The critique of monogamy is deeply rooted in feminist and queer theoretical traditions that have challenged dominant relational norms since the 1970s. Feminist scholar Adrienne Rich, in her seminal essay *Compulsory Heterosexuality and Lesbian Existence* (1983), argued that heterosexuality is socially enforced through cultural, economic, and institutional mechanisms. Rich illuminated how lesbian existence—and by extension, any identity outside heterosexuality—is marginalized, invalidated, or erased within this framework. These mechanisms perpetuate a "heterosexual matrix," wherein relationships conform to rigid gender roles and heterosexual partnerships are upheld as the primary or only valid form of sexual and relational expression. This prioritization of heterosexual monogamy aligns closely with mononormativity, which similarly upholds monogamy as the standard or ideal for all relationships, regardless of sexual orientation.

Audre Lorde (1984) expanded on these critiques by exploring the intersections of sexuality, identity, and systemic oppression. Lorde's work highlighted how societal norms around sexuality and relational structures intersect with race, class, and gender, creating layers of marginalization. As a Black lesbian, Lorde challenged the normative expectations of femininity, heterosexuality, and monogamy, offering a deeply intersectional critique of how social institutions—such as family, religion, and education—enforce these norms. Her contributions emphasized the interconnectedness of hetero- and mononormativity, underscoring their role in upholding systemic oppression and exclusionary frameworks.

Despite legal advances such as the legalization of same-sex marriage in Canada in 2005 and the USA in 2015, relational norms remain constrained by mononormativity. As Rubin (1984) observed, monogamous relationships are often positioned as inherently superior to other relational structures, such as polyamory, open relationships, or swinging. This privilege of monogamy is reinforced through media narratives, cultural expectations, and legal frameworks, which collectively marginalize and stigmatize non-monogamous practices. The cultural dominance of monogamy continues to shape the relational and sex therapy field, where therapists and researchers often assume monogamy as the default relational model.

Critical feminist theorists, including bell hooks (1984), Audre Lorde (1984), and Sara Ahmed (2017), have drawn attention to the systemic roots of these normative structures. They argue that hetero- and mononormativity are deeply intertwined with colonialism, patriarchy, white supremacy, and cultural imperialism. These systems create and perpetuate hierarchies that marginalize 2SLGBTQ+ and BIPOC communities, as well as those who engage in non-monogamous relationships. Ahmed, in particular, emphasizes the importance of deconstructing normative frameworks to create inclusive and equitable spaces for diverse identities and relational forms. Her work highlights the necessity of challenging assumptions about relational "ideals" as a form of activism both inside and outside therapeutic spaces.

In the field of relational and sex therapy, these critiques demand a reflexive examination of the ways in which mono- and heteronormative discourses shape therapeutic practices. My own process of untangling from traditional training has involved applying feminist and queer theory to disrupt and deconstruct these norms. As I reflect on the therapeutic field's engagement with monogamy, I pose critical questions: How does mononormativity manifest in therapeutic contexts? How do these norms influence the understanding of relational well-being? By building on the work of feminist and queer theorists, this paper aims to examine how mono- and heteronormative assumptions continue to shape research and practice in the relational and sex therapy field.

The mono-hetero normative discourse with human sexuality and relationship therapy research

My application of social justice principles begins with critically examining who is being referenced and represented in research, theory, and practice. It also involves questioning how these references and representations are depicted. What dominant narratives are being reinforced, and what subjugated stories are excluded or erased? By interrogating these dynamics, therapists can uncover the underlying assumptions that shape the field and take intentional steps to validate diverse experiences.

For instance, applying Rubin's *Charmed Circle* theory in therapy involves recognizing and affirming clients' diverse sexual identities and practices. Rubin (1984) illustrated how societal norms categorize certain sexual behaviors and relationship structures as "good" or "normal" while marginalizing others as "bad" or "deviant." In therapeutic practice, this means working to dismantle these harmful dichotomies by creating space for clients to explore their identities and desires without judgment. A practical intervention might include normalizing discussions around non-monogamous relationship structures or supporting clients in challenging internalized shame about their sexual practices. This approach not only promotes inclusivity but also empowers clients to define relational and sexual fulfillment on their own terms.

The pervasiveness of hetero- and mononormative discourses begins early in life, as seen in social conditioning through seemingly innocuous childhood chants like, "K-I-S-S-I-N-G, first comes love, then comes marriage, then comes baby in the baby carriage." This simple rhyme encapsulates deeply ingrained societal expectations about relationships, sexuality, and life trajectories, reinforcing the belief that a meaningful and fulfilling relational life must follow a specific sequence. This concept aligns with Gahran's (2017) "relationship escalator," which outlines a normative progression of monogamous relationships as a societal ideal.

Gahran identifies eight stages on the relationship escalator:

1. **Making Contact** – Initial casual encounters, flirting, or hooking up.
2. **Initiation** – Emotional investment and courtship involving expressions of love and physical affection.
3. **Claiming and Defining** – Mutual declarations of love, presenting as a couple, and establishing exclusivity.
4. **Establishment** – Developing routines and shared activities, including sexual intimacy.
5. **Commitment** – Planning a future together, merging families of origin, and mutual accountability.
6. **Merging** – Sharing finances, living arrangements, and formalizing the relationship through engagement or similar commitments.
7. **Conclusion** – Legal recognition of the relationship (e.g., marriage) with an implied permanence.
8. **Legacy** – Often marked by societal expectations to have children, purchase property, and continue the generational cycle.

In therapy, the "relationship escalator" provides a lens to critique how societal norms influence clients' relational expectations and experiences. For example, therapists can help clients deconstruct the pressure to conform to these sequential steps and validate alternative relational paths that might better align with their values and desires. A therapist informed by social justice might ask: How does the escalator model shape your understanding of success in relationships? Do these expectations reflect your personal goals, or are they rooted in societal conditioning?

Such interventions help clients identify and challenge the ways in which mono- and heteronormative discourses impact their relationships and well-being. By applying social justice frameworks, therapists can foster an environment where clients feel empowered to explore and embrace relational structures—whether monogamous, polyamorous, or otherwise—that honor their authentic selves. In doing so, therapy becomes a site of both personal transformation and resistance to dominant norms.

The relationship escalator's prevalence in both cultural and academic discourses underscores its role in perpetuating these normative ideals. In the next section, I will demonstrate how these assumptions are embedded within the field of relational and sex therapy and explore the implications for therapeutic practice.

Mononormativity in Relationship Models

The escalator metaphor is steeped in developmental, relational, and family cycle models (Erikson,1950;1968; Carter & McGoldrick,1980; 1988; 1999; Knapp, 1978). Models that continue to play a central role in informing research and practice in the sex, "marriage/couple," and family therapy fields. Couple-privileged models focus on the milestones or transitions involved in developing and maintaining "functioning" dyadic intimate (romantic/sexual) relationships. According to Nichols (1988, 1996), the success of the marital couple in a therapeutic process is in their relational ability to fulfill the following five tasks: 1) *commitment* to be in and to maintain the relationship; 2) demonstrate *caring* as a form of emotional attachment they have for each other and the ability to express respect; 3) *communication* ability to develop a pattern of verbal and nonverbal communication to share meaning and construct a shared universe; 4) *conflict and compromise,* or their ability to identify and manage their disagreements and emotional injuries, including how effective they are at compromising and resolving conflict; and 5) *Contract,* or the agreement to be a couple and establish a mutually satisfying affectional and sexual relationship. The "couple" has become the archetype of relational and sexual fulfillment, which has been well documented in research (see Byers, 2005; Schoenfeld et al., 2017). Dyadic-focused research continues to demonstrate a strong association between sexual satisfaction and relationship satisfaction, indicating people who are sexually satisfied in their relationship are likely to have a high level of satisfaction with their relationship overall (Byers & Wang, 2004; Christopher & Sprecher, 2000; Fallis et al., 2016). Embedded is the assumption that romantic-sexual bonding with another person is not only expected of the "normal" and "healthy" developmental stage, but it becomes a marker of success to continue in the monogamous structure.

Applying social justice and activism includes challenging normative assumptions across different domains (Ahmed, 2017). In this case, the relational connection and intimacy normative discourse. We are encouraged to rethink how relational norms are constructed and how they impact various forms of identity (e.g., being in a sexual/romantic relationship with another person) and social interaction (e.g., engaging in sexual/romantic activities). In other words, how does this "normative relational model" deny gay men in open relationships a sense of commitment with partners? How limiting are the ideas and practice of contracting and communicating for folx in polyamory relationships? Applying Ahmed's critiques of normative structures, emotional regulation, and the politics of visibility provides valuable insights for understanding and challenging normative assumptions about monogamous relationships and sexuality. The application of a social justice approach creates more space and understanding for diverse relational structures and a range of connections and meaning in various relational configurations, which in turn potentially leads to more visibility and acceptance. Challenging mononormativity is an active process of critical thinking in various research domains, including that of the sexuality realm.

Built on the works of Masters and Johnson, the dyadic structure also remains at the center of sex therapy research and practice. This is most notoriously evident in their ground-breaking research and the development of the Human Sexual Response Model (Masters & Johnson, 1966). To this day, this model remains the bedrock and most influential source of "sexual functioning" in sex therapy. The model was developed and founded on the pairing of cisgender men and women. The couple was either married to each other and/or the participant was willing to engage in vaginal-penile intercourse with another person regardless of relational status. This model is based on 694 participants, 97% were white, 80% were between the age of 18-40 years, and 70% had college, university and/or postgraduate education. You read that correctly— what we refer to as "normal sexual functioning" is based on heterosexual intercourse with predominantly younger adults in the midwest United States during the early and mid-1960s. If you are realizing that you and/or many people you know are not represented in this dominant model of sexuality, you are not alone. Given how many sexual human beings exist and the variation of billions of people in the world, how is it that this remains the golden standard model of human sexual response? Challenging what is defined as "normal" and who defines normalcy is a crucial process in a social justice approach.

Research Bias and the Mythical Norm

These sexual and relational models are depictions of what Audre Lorde (1984) identified as the *mythical norm,* which at the time of her writing was defined as "white, thin, male, young, heterosexual, Christian and financially secure" (p.116). To this list I add able-bodied and cisgendered. The mythical norm operates invisibly as the default in society, making those who fit this norm less aware of their privilege and are usually centered as the reference point to what becomes normal. People whose identity categories align with this norm are often not required to think about their identity categories (e.g., race, gender, sexual orientation, relational orientation) because these traits are normalized. More applicable is that most research, theorizing, and intervening are tailored to this group (i.e. monogamous relationships). The identity categories of the "mythical norm" are the ones most represented in relational and sex research in the USA and Canada.

This research practice remains prevalent to this day partly because of the access to undergraduate students as research participants. Some researchers have drawn attention to how problematic claims about human psychology and behaviour based on Western, Educated, Industrialized, Rich, and Democratic (WEIRD) societies are generalized across human populations (Henrich et al., 2010). These WEIRD research samples are not representative nor universal. I consider this research process highly unjust and an indicator of the sanction for colonial practices of knowledge production and domination within both our professional bodies and academic institutions which conduct research and train many professionals.

How do we reconcile that the evidence-based science many of us defend and protect tends to represent *and* potentially benefit the most privileged in our sociopolitical and cultural context? The impact of the research findings and efficiency of treatment that informs clinical practice, in turn, continues to benefit the people it represents. Ethically and from a justice perspective, I also need to ask: How is what we know about a very selective group of people not harming others? For example, ideas about sexual responses that pathologize people having sexual dysfunctions. What is the impact of research and "clinical standards" that do not account for the unique differences of the people who are rendered invisible by not being included in the production and construction of knowledge? For example, for people with a range of physical disabilities, sexual pleasure practices, and sexual and gender minorities who might not center vaginal-penile intercourse in their sexually fulfilled lives.

If there is a temptation to start to defend and contextual research that is 40, 50, or 60 years old with the excuse that they did not know better, now ask, what is the rationale— the "excuse"— to continue this practice today? Most of the sex-related and relationship-focused research tends to be concentrated on heterosexual and cisgendered dyadic structures. Despite my critiques and invitations to researchers at academic research conferences to start with more inclusive rep-resentation and to be clearer about who benefits and who does not from these findings (De Santis, 2011; De Santis, 2014; Sakulak & De Santis, 2016). Research practices that continue to replicate and reinforce the same system under the guise of the "scientific method" continue the practice of colonialism and imperialism that leads to the institutionalization of white supremacy: the nuclear family contributing to the mono- and heteronormative discourse.

Rubin (1984) presented a systemic structure that depicts sexual expressions, practices, behaviours, identities, and configurations that are socially condoned, promoted, and privileged and those which are condemned, discriminated, and marginalized. According to Rubin, sex and sexuality are either considered normal, good, natural, blessed, holy, and healthy, or abnormal, bad, unnatural, demanded, sinful, and sick. She explains how sexuality, eroticism and identity are regulated and valued in our social world within a Western cultural (primarily American moral) context. I find Rubin's work helpful in navigating social justice-oriented conversations about how sexuality and relationship structures are promoted, rewarded, and regulated. Using the Charmed Circle, she depicts identities, behaviours, and configurations that organize sexuality that is procreative, heterosexual, and monogamous. Sexuality between two married mix-gender/sex people only who are approximately similar in age and engage in primarily penis-vaginal intercourse within private quarters is privileged, protected, and valued.

Any other sexual practices are not afforded social approval (and, at times, social and legal protection). Behaviours (anal sex), relationship configurations (threesomes), and identities (Lesbian) that are situated outside of the charmed circle are categorized negatively, stigmatized, and pathologized. These outer limits would include sexual activity that is considered queer, kinky, or pleasure-focused, includes sex toys, is experienced solo or with multiple partners either at the same time or concurrently, casual, paid, involves sexually explicit material, and/or takes place in public spaces/sex parties. Rubin (1984) also explicitly articulated the hierarchy of sex and sexuality into superior/inferior dichotomies where the line is drawn between normal and abnormal, healthy and unhealthy, and natural and unnatural. For example, although heterosexuality is the archetype of coupling, a married heterosexual couple is seen as more superior than a common-law heterosexual couple, yet both are more superior than a queer couple. Similarly, a queer couple who are sexually exclusive is considered above a mix-gender/sex couple hooking up for a threesome. Rubin's sex hierarchy also underscores binary constructs of gender, highlighting the pathologization of non-binary gender. In practice, applying Rubin's Charmed Circle theory means recognizing and validating clients' diverse sexual identities and practices, thus promoting inclusivity in therapeutic settings. In analyzing current practices, we must delve into the theoretical frameworks that underpin traditional therapy models, questioning their relevance and inclusivity.

Case Studies and Practical Applications

My experience in the relational and sex therapy field is that a similar dichotomous structure prevails in what is considered therapeutic success. Generally speaking, it involves creating a bubble around two people (depending on the degree of openness and acceptance from the therapist, all genders and sexual orientations are welcomed, acknowledged and valid). The dyadic privilege, however, is embedded in our field - it orients our work! Consider the name of the leading organizations: the American Association of Marriage and Family Therapy (AAMFT) and the Canadian Association of Marriage and Family Therapy (CAMFT), which recently changed their name to the Canadian Association of Couple and Family Therapy and voted down using "relational" instead of "couple," and the theories, models (attachment, interdependence, relational dialectics theory, social exchange), and training programs involved in the accreditation and certification of relational and sex therapists such as the Association of Sex Therapy in Ontario (ASTO formerly BESTCO), Gottman Method Couples Therapy, and Emotionally Focused Couples Therapy (EFT). Dr. John Gottman, Co-founder of The Gottman Institute, and Susan Johnson, Director of the International Centre of Excellence in Emotionally Focused Therapy, are two very influential relationship researchers and practitioners who offer training and certification in their respective therapy models. Among the various sex therapist supervisees I have worked with, about 80% either have Emotionally Focused Therapy (EFT) or Gottman method couple therapy training. Currently, the most influential models that inform intimate relating and connecting are based on research on couples. Monogamy is unquestioned as the default.

Dismantling monogamy as an application of social justice is both understanding how we got here and understanding what is needed to move on from a structure and relational process that can be limiting, oppressive, and dismissive of clients' range of meaningful lived experiences. As a sex and relational therapist, I constantly need to ask myself what I need to undo for clients' clinical care. What forms of activism are needed from me in the research field to reflect the clients I work with and the concerns they bring forward regarding their sexualities, sexual expressions, relational processes, and structures? How do I engage as a politicized research practitioner to advocate for interventions and processes that are accessible and beneficial to all citizens regardless of their relational status and identity?

Social Justice in Relational and Sex Therapy Practice

Politicized practitioners assert that the practice of therapy is not a neutral process. Baines (2017) writes, "Social work is not a neutral, caring profession, but an active political process," indicating there is "no politics-free-zone" (p. 7). Brown and Augusta-Scott (2007) state that to "not unpack, or deconstruct, dominant stories are to leave dominance, social discourses, and social relations of power intact" (p. xi). Therefore, therapy is a political process. I would argue this is the case for all practitioners (and researchers) regardless of professional orientation (and ontology). I agree that regardless of professional orientation and clinical occupation, ranging from nursing to psychotherapy and everything in between— including working with clients, clinical training, supervising, and conducting research—we are not neutral!

For Reynolds and Hammoud-Beckett (2018), social justice activism and therapy must include a "critical resistance toward neutrality and objectivity" while "resisting and transforming the structures in society that create conditions for oppression and exploitation." They ask the following questions: "How are the politics of neutrality and objectivity mapped onto the legacies of white supremacy and colonization in the helping professions? How are professional objectivity and neutrality connected to other sites of oppression and exclusion?" (p. 5). Earlier, I demonstrated how sex therapy and relational research have contributed to upholding a structural system that continues to benefit the most privileged in Canada and the USA (mostly white, young, and educated heterosexuals). I will now turn my attention to the therapeutic context, which includes clinical training, supervision, and client meetings facilitated by relational and sex therapy. In this context, therapeutic conversations are *both* political processes, *and* all participating members are active political actors (Baines, 2017). Neither clients, therapists, supervisees, nor supervisors have a "neutral" positionality within our multi-contextual social structures. We all bring our multiple axes of identities to these interactions. As I see it, the choice for politicized practitioners is to either challenge the status quo or support it regardless of positionality. Either way, the choice we make has an impact on clinical care. Considering Reynold and Hammoud-Beckett's words, how are we contributing to clients' experiences of oppression and exclusion in the practice and training of sex and relational therapists?

Challenges and Opportunities in Dismantling Monogamy

In the field of sex and relational therapy, assumptions, frameworks, and models that uphold mono-normativity are dominant and, as a result, are politically active rather than neutral. The dominant discourse in the field promotes and privileges monogamy as the means to relational and sexual fulfilment. We need to be very cautious about how accessing and applying these models can potentially be oppressive and exclusionary of clients' experiences. As a systematically trained therapist, I think of clients in their various relational systems, which include a myriad of relationships with friends, partners, lovers, members of their family of origin and family of choice. These vast relationships take place in a range of contexts and are simultaneously intertwined with larger systems (culture) and structures (legal). I position myself similarly to Iasenza (2020), whose theoretical framework is informed by early training as a family (relational) therapist and that internalized pathologizing sexual narratives is problematic and can be transformed. This transformation is another way social justice is practiced. Sexual narratives exist in and outside clients, therapists, supervisors, and researchers. Sexual narratives are part and parcel of the dominant hetero- and mono-normative discourse that has tyrannized many of our clients (perhaps even ourselves) and access to a meaningful and vibrant erotic life. Dominant sexual narrative lay on top of Rubin's Charm Circle, in which some sexual acts and relational structures are deemed "abnormal" and are pathologized.

Engaging Clients in Conversations about Monogamy

I have found facilitating conversations with clients about their sexual narratives (more specifically with their experiences with the concepts of intimacy, connection, self-determination, sexuality, sensuality, eroticism, vulnerability, desires, and pleasure) to be some of the most sensitive and sacred exchanges. These intricate dialogues are complex and underscore how human beings are meaning-making creatures (Rosen,1996). An application of social justice creates space for me to engage with both personal narratives and dominant social discourses critically. I challenge dominant and primarily unquestioned or un-questionable "truths" about human sexualities, sexual functioning, relationship satisfaction and fulfillment that dominant research practice and therapy models endorse and prescribe. By challenging these dominant notions, generative therapeutic conversations about alternative possibilities can take place. This process can be affirming for clients as they can experience inclusion and value. Their participation and engagement in these conversations are part of their process of sexual and relational emancipation. Together, we can create new meanings about their sexuality and, if desired, make a relational paradigm shift that is not restricted to monogamy (Zambrano, 1999).

My therapeutic conversations are not scripted. I am unable to out-line a neat and linear sequence of questions to "produce an outcome." Conversations with clients and supervisees are just that – conversations about how we know what we know, what we are curious about exploring further, and what can be imaginable, risky, and necessary. It includes generative conversations about possibilities of what could be different and how changes could take place. In more concrete terms, I attempt to have conversations about the terrain of relationality and sexuality that have been traditionally governed around monogamy, typically in conjunction with heterosexuality. In collaboration with clients, we deconstruct the mono- and heteronormative discourse about sexual and relational fulfillment.

About 15 years ago, I started to ask more questions about relational structures and choices around being single. For example, I asked clients who came in individually about how they chose to organize their relational lives with family and friends. I asked if they had any interest in and/or had experiences with other forms of relationships that might include variations of intimacy and closeness with their minds, hearts, and bodies. However, many clients appeared confused at first as I unpacked the questions and indicated that for some people, these relationships could fall under deep, meaningful, close friendships that might or might not also include romance and sexuality, as well as occasional or one-time encounters. I would emphasize that not everyone wants to be "partnered" and that being single is not problematic. I can still recall the few clients who took a double take. It was less about being confused about what I was asking and more curious if I was opening up space for a conversation that rarely had taken place for them in a therapeutic context. The experience of liberation was palpable. Involved in a therapeutic conversation that did not problematize because of their relational preferences.

For some clients, the conversations about mono-normativity invited them to reflect on their experiences with social gatherings (i.e., dinner parties) arranged by friends who were couple-oriented, and an invite would only be extended when another "single person" would be there. Their experiences of marginalization would open a door that might lead them to question themselves. I found it was important to ensure that clients were able to discern how dominant discourse was in operation and that our social structures reinforced them when not challenged and dismantled. When we could hold a critical analysis of mono-normativity, I would come to learn more about clients and how they had and accessed high-quality and meaningful relationships that were centered around romance, sexuality, or domesticity. I would often reflect on what I would hear regarding their experience of a meaningful life — albeit different from the social norm. During those moments, I realized, they realized, I was acknowledging their existence — their preferred way of being. That involvement of witnessing someone's experience of being seen more fully is part of the power of therapy. These acts of inclusion are only one facet of social justice in action. The dialogue between us revealed how rare of an occurrence this was for them. Outside the therapeutic context, some clients began to advocate for themselves, create communities, and work with co-conspirators to challenge the discourse and social structures that denied them access as either a single person and/or someone who had multiple relationships.

It was an analogous reaction to what I had experienced 30 years ago (and still do) when I would ask a similar question about dating or being in relationships: at that time, I would ask, Do you tend to date women, men, or both? When met with some surprise, I would state that making assumptions would not be helpful and that I hoped the client would feel completely welcome and speak freely about all parts of their relational and sexual lives. I would add that all people were welcome to work with me and that I believed there was a range of identities. Some non-queer clients took the opportunity to ask more questions about their limited knowledge and experience with queer folks. Many clients expressed gratitude for the opportunity to ask their questions without experiencing judgment. Regardless of clients' identities, relational status, and sexual experiences and practices, I found that having these conversations was another way to practice social justice. Albeit invited by the client, it allowed us together to critically question the structures and systems that prescribe and regulate human sexualities, behaviour, and relational configuration. Clients started to recognize their unearned privilege and how they benefited from the ways heterosexism, cisgenderism, sexism, and patriarchy, while others, specifically members of sexual, gender, and relationship minority groups, experienced oppression.

As a politicized practitioner, conversations about sexuality generated opportunities for conversations about mono-normativity and other axes of oppression (e.g., race, religion, income, language, and marital status) that brought forward access to power and resources. Who gets treated with respect and dignity and who is rendered non-human (Butler, 2004). These conversations that took place in a therapeutic context appeared to create more understanding and acceptance of a range of human existence (theirs and others), expanding clients' ideas about a meaningful relational and sexual life that may appear different than the majority. More recently, clients cautiously engaged in conversations that question monogamy as the only way to organize one's sexuality and relationality. Regardless of which of these sexual and relational topics we focused on, I experienced clients' engagement in these difficult and heartfelt conversations to be very courageous, vulnerable, and genuine. It represented a willingness that clients wanted to learn more and be open about practices outside of their lived experience. I noticed it also brought some relief and self-acceptance to other clients who felt valued and acknowledged.

I now ask follow-up questions about clients' choices and preferences about being in relation with other people and what they choose to include in these relationships. It might or might not include sex and/or romance, emotional and/or physical closeness— I have learned I cannot assume, and by asking open questions, the specifics and nuances of how clients organize their lives are illuminating. I have come to appreciate that sometimes clients have done all the dismantling of monogamy; my job is to ensure I don't impose the constraint of monogamy and compulsory heterosexuality on them. I ask about the role gender plays in these relationships and how important it is for them. I include questions about their interest in relationships, and if they are in relationships, I ask about their preference to have one relationship at a time, compared to more than one, regardless of relationship duration and frequency of seeing other people. If clients present as a two-some, I ask about their relational structure and if there are other consensual partners and/or other meaningful relationships that would be helpful to note in our work together. When there are more partners or people involved, I ask about the degree of involvement in their lives and their relationship agreements among all members. I ask monogamous clients about their current arrangements and if they were deliberately negotiated. These types of inquiries are another facet of being a politicized practitioner dismantling monogamy. It requires that I do not make monogamy the default. I deliberately hold space for people to define what type of relationships are more meaningful for them, how they prefer to organize their relational lives, and if these were intentional choices or if they were following socially prescribed expectations. I am not invested in promoting one structure over the other. What I am interested in is ensuring I am not participating in continuing to uphold ideologies that contribute to oppressive structural systems that limit clients' well-being and dignity.

As a sex therapist, I aim to ask questions about how they experience pleasure and erotic fulfillment with themselves and with others if that is how they also practice. I attempt to move away from the genital-focus measurement of function. I ask about their desires, fantasies, and experiences. I have worked with many clients who have expressed concerns (and, at times, distress) about their current relational and sexual practices not being "normal." Their concerns and distress are very real, impacting their personal and relational well-being. These conversations are very sensitive, and I need to balance the client's lived experiences, which include what is being said and unsaid, the impact of these experiences on the clients' resources and to what degree and type of change is possible with my application of social justice. Therapeutic conversations are different from a lecture on oppressive structure in our social world. Clients are not signing up to be lectured; therapeutic conversation needs to focus on what is important to clients. It is their agenda for change we respond to while simultaneously engaging critically about the structural, cultural, and family systems that are embedded in our lives, even when belonging seems impossible. It has meant that internal and external expectations need to be reviewed, revised, and sometimes relinquished.

Training and Supervision in Non-Monogamous Practices

Gayle Rubin's (1984) "charmed circle" remains a useful frame for comprehending which sexualities and relational structures continue to be marginalized and experience discrimination. Not only do I share her work with clients, but I also bring Rubin's work into supervision and training with fledging sex and relational therapists. I invite them to consider how they think about and work with clients. I encourage them to consider their frame of reference about sexuality and relationship structures. Supervisees are encouraged to reflect on what ideas they move toward and away from, reminding them there is never a neutral positionality as therapists. I invite them to consider if they are explicitly and/or unintentionally organizing the "therapy" within a mono-normative frame and what the implications are during the therapeutic process and the clients' experience. I encourage them to question how the human sexual response model limits their therapeutic conversation, not only their work with non-binary and trans folks but also cisgender people. More so, I invite them to consider how the models are researched, who benefits from their use, and who could potentially be harmed if they are not critically considered. All of the supervisees and students I have worked with are committed to being ethical practitioners; some already claim to be politicized practitioners who participate in activism and social justice, while others do not consider therapeutic conversations as a political process. Not all therapists are activists, but they all are influential and hold positions of power in their relationships with their clients. How they tend to and use their power is important to know. Here are a few questions I ask supervisees to consider when paying attention to mono-normative discourse: What language do you use to ask clients about themselves, their relationships, and their identities? What are the underlying assumptions in your intake and assessment questions? What do you base them on? And what is the purpose of these questions? Do your therapeutic questions open up space for clients to bring forward less occurring ways they express, identify, and behave sexually and relationally?

Moving Towards Inclusive Practice

It is with a mix of embarrassment, humility, and openness that I declare my current social justice practice today carries earlier versions of myself over the past five decades; this perspective also reveals both my growth and current limitations. I suspect that these shortcomings are connected to acquiring access to positions of power and privilege in education, training, and clinical practice, which wreak havoc on a 360-degree practice of social justice. This, however, does not grant me a pass. Instead, I believe the access and positionality to power and privilege demand that I engage in critical self-reflection and self-interrogation (CSR/SI). Ken Hardy (2016) states that the process of CSR/SI is necessary when we have conversations about class, gender, race, sexual orientation, and dimensions of social identity/category with clients and supervisees. Once again, I find myself influenced by another of Baines's (2017) core concepts of social justice and anti-oppressive practice; it is essential that we, as clinicians (and, I would add as supervisors), engage in "self-reflexive practice and ongoing social analysis" (p. 8) as part of the therapeutic process and use our range of experiences to contribute to on-going theory and therapeutic practice.

References

Ahmed, S. (2017). *Living a feminist life.* Duke.

Baines, D. (2017). Anti-oppressive practice: Roots, theory, tensions. In D. Baines (Ed) *Doing anti-oppressive practice: Social justice social work,* 3rd ed.) (pp. 2-29). Fernwood.

Brown, C. and Augusta-Scott, T. (2007). Introduction: Postmodernism, reflexivity, and narrative therapy. In C. Brown and T. Augusta-Scott (Eds.) *Narrative therapy* (pp. ix-xliii). Sage.

Butler, J. (2004). Undoing gender. Routledge.

Byers, S. (2005) Relationship satisfaction and sexual satisfaction: a longitudinal study of individuals in long-term relationships. *Journal of Sex Research.* 42: 113-8. DOI: 10.1080/00224490509552264

Byers, S., & Wang, A. (2004). Understanding sexuality in close relationships from the social exchange perspective. In J. H. Harvey, A. Wenzel, & S. Sprecher (Eds.), *The handbook of sexuality in close relationships* (pp. 203–234). Lawrence Erlbaum Associates Publishers.

Carter, B., & McGoldrick, M. (Eds.). (1988). *The changing family life cycle: A framework for family therapy* (2nd ed.). Gardner Press. (pp. 3-28). Allyn and Bacon

Carter, B. & McGoldrick, M. (1999). Overview: The expanded family life cycle. In B. Carter & M. McGoldrick (Eds.). *The expanded family life cycle, 3rd ed* (pp. 1-26). Allyn and Bacon

Christopher, F.S. and Sprecher, S. (2000), Sexuality in Marriage, Dating, and Other Relationships: A Decade Review. *Journal of Marriage and Family, 62,* 999-1017. https://doi.org/10.1111/j.1741-3737.2000.00999.x

De Santis C. (October, 2015). Theorizing sexuality: Can sexuality studies be polyamorous? Presentation for *Canadian Sex Research Forum,* Kelowna, BC.

De Santis, C. (September, 2011). Research Conundrum: Inclusivity. Presentation for the *Canadian Sex Research Forum,* Vancouver, BC.

Erikson, E. H. (1950). *Childhood and society.* New York: Norton.

Erikson, E. H. (1968). *Identity: Youth and crisis.* New York: Norton.

Erikson E. H. (1982). *The life cycle completed.* New York: W.W. Norton & Company.

Fallis, E., Rehman, U., Woody, E., & Purdon C. (2016). The longitudinal association of relationship satisfaction and sexual satisfaction in long-term relationships. *Journal of Family Psychology, 7,* 822-831. DOI: 10.1037/fam0000205.

Gahran, A. (2017). *Stepping off the relationship escalator: Uncommon love and life*. Off the Escalator Enterprises: Boulder, Colorado.

Gottman, J. (1999). *The marriage clinic*. Norton.

Hardy, K. & Bobes, T. (2016). Core competencies for executing culturally sensitive supervision and training. In K. Hardy & T. Bobes (Eds). Culturally sensitive supervision training, (pp. 11-15). Routledge.

hooks, b. (2010). *Teaching critical thinking*. Routledge.

Henrich, J., Heine, S. J. & Norenzayan, A. (2010). The weirdest people in the world? Behavioral and Brain Science, 33, 61–83.

Iasenza. S. (2020). *Transforming sexual narratives: A relational approach to sex therapy*. Routledge.

Jackson, S. and Scott, S. (2004). The personal is still political: heterosexuality, feminism and monogamy. *Feminism & Psychology,* 14 (1) 151-157.

Johnson, S. (2004). *The practice of emotionally focused couple therapy (2nd ed)*. Brunner-Routledge.

Kaplan, R. (1992). Compulsory heterosexuality and the bisexual existence: Toward a bisexual feminist understanding of heterosexism. In R. Weise (Ed). *Closer to home: Bisexuality and feminism.* (pp 269-80). Seal Press.

Knapp, M. L. (1978). *Social intercourse: From greeting to goodbye*. Allyn & Bacon.

Lewis, D. (2005). Against the grain: Black women and sexuality. *Agenda: Empowering Women for Gender Equity, 63,* 11–24.

Lorde, A. (1984). *Sister Outsider, Essay and Speeches.* The Crossing Press.

Masters, W. & Johnson, V. (1966). *Human sexual response*. Little Brown.

Nichols, W. C. (1988). *Marital therapy: An integrative approach*. Guilford.

Nichols, W. C. (1996). *Treating people in families: An integrative framework*.Guilford

Nichols, W. C. (1997). Integrative marital therapy. In F. D. Dattilio (Ed.), Integrative cases in couples and family therapy: A cognitive-behavioral perspective (pp. 233–256). Guilford.

Pieper, M. & Bauer, R. (2005). Call for Papers: International Conference on Polyamory and Mono-normativity- Research Centre for Feminist, Gender & Queer Studies, University of Hamburg, November 5th/6th 2005.

Rich, A. (1980). Compulsory heterosexuality and Lesbian existence. *Signs: Journal of Women in Culture and Society, 5,* 631-660.

Rosa, B. (1994). Anti-monogamy: A radical challenge to compulsory heterosexuality. In G. Griffin, M. Fiesta, S. Rai & S. Roseneil, (Eds.)., *Stirring it,* (pp. 107-120). Routledge.

Rosen, H. (1996). Meaning-making narratives: Foundations for constructivist and social constructionist psychotherapies. In H. Rosen & K. Kuehlwein (Eds). *Constructing realities* (pp. 3-51). Jossey-Bass.

Reynolds, V. and Hammoud-Beckett, S. (2018). Social justice activism and therapy: Tensions, points of connection, and hopeful scepticism. In C. Audet and D. Paré (Eds). *Social justice and counseling* (pp. 3-15). NY: Routledge.

Rubin, G. (1984). Think sex: Notes for a radical theory of the politics of sexuality. In C. Vance (Ed). *Pleasure and Danger* (pp. 267-319). Pandora.

Salaluk. J. & De Santis, C. (September, 2016). Exclusion of Sexual Minority Group Members from Sexual Science: Estimates, Critiques, and Ways Forward. Oral presentation for *Canadian Sex Research Forum*, Quebec City, Quebec.

Schippers, M. (2016). Beyond monogamy. NY: NewYork University Press

Schoenfeld, E. A., Loving, T. J., Pope, M. T., Huston, T. L., & Stulhofer, A. (2017). Does sex really matter? Examining the connections between spouses' nonsexual behaviors, sexual frequency, sexual satisfaction, and marital satisfaction. *Archives of Sexual Behavior, 46*, 489-501. https://doi.org/10.1007/s10508-015-0672-4

Stelboum, J. (1999). Patriarchal monogamy. In M. Munson and J. Stelboum (Eds.). *The Lesbian polyamory reader* (pp. 39-46). Harrington.

Taylor, P.S. (2018). The marriage secret: It makes you richer and happier. Macleans. https://macleans.ca/society/life/the-marriage-secret-it-makes-you-richer-and-happier/

Zambrano M. (1999) Paradigms of polyamory. *Journal of Lesbian Studies, 3*, 151-5. https://doi:10.1300/J155v03n01_16

Field Placements and Clinical Programs Must Integrate Anti-Oppressive Perspectives and Psychodynamic Theory. Here's Why.

RAHIM THAWER, MSW, RSW

In 2011, within the walls of a graduate classroom, a debate sparked a transformative journey in my understanding of psychotherapeutic modalities. The question at hand was whether anti-oppressive psychotherapy stood as a modality in its own right. As a fervent advocate, my response resounded with a clear affirmation. Fast forward 10 years, and the landscape of my perspective has undergone a seismic shift. Today, while I steadfastly employ an anti-oppression lens, my practice is a tapestry woven from the intricate threads of psychodynamic, cognitive-behavioral, and Gestalt therapies. This evolution is reflective of a broader, critical conversation in the field—a dialogue that recognizes the indispensability of integrating varied therapeutic approaches to truly address the multi-faceted nature of mental health.

It's crucial to consider the contemporary relevance of psychodynamic theory within clinical social work. Thyer (2015) challenges the traditional linkage between clinical social work and psychodynamic theory, arguing for a re-evaluation of its role in light of evidence-based practices. He posits that clinging to historical theoretical frameworks may hinder progress and calls instead for a modern redefinition of clinical social work that is unshackled from its historical ties to psychodynamic theory.

In this paper, I embark on an exploratory analysis of six inherent tensions I've encountered as a clinical supervisor, particularly when supervisees align exclusively with an anti-oppressive approach, often sidelining psychoanalytic contributions as antiquated methodologies. The dissection of these tensions is more than an academic exercise; it is an imperative to bridge the theoretical divides that, if left unchecked, risk compartmentalizing clinical practices to the detriment of the rich, nuanced care our clients deserve. It is here, at the intersection of anti-oppressive perspectives and psychodynamic theory, that this paper finds its purpose.

Background

The roots of my observations stem from my role as a clinical supervisor for graduate students, where I've noticed a pronounced trend: Master of Social Work (MSW) students are increasingly politicized, keenly aware of the marginalization and systemic violence that our clients endure. This awareness is markedly less evident among applicants from Counselling Psychology programs. One could speculate that this divergence arises from the pedagogical focus of MSW training in Canada, which prioritizes the instillation of a robust anti-oppression analysis, often at the expense of deep engagement with psychotherapeutic techniques.

As we consider the educational focus in MSW training, Lee & Rasmussen (2019) provide an insightful perspective on psychodynamic contributions to understanding power dynamics and institutional factors in social work practice. They explore how psychodynamic theories can be adapted to address issues of diversity and power, offering a valuable lens through which practitioners can better understand and navigate the complexities of the sociopolitical realities affecting clients.

The anti-oppressive lens that social workers bring to the clinical front lines is undeniably valuable; it prepares them to navigate the complex sociopolitical waters in which our clients often find themselves adrift. However, there exists a palpable gap—a lacuna that separates these broad contextual principles from the foundational psychodynamic concepts that are equally pivotal in the nuanced landscape of individual psychotherapy. This disconnect not only hinders the holistic understanding of client experiences but also limits the therapeutic toolkit available to practitioners.

Conversely, students with a psychodynamic orientation may have a propensity to over-individualize problems, potentially overlooking the influential social context that shapes client experiences. While they are adept at navigating the internal worlds of their clients, there is a risk of minimizing the external forces at play—forces that are often as impactful as the psychological undercurrents.

The confluence of these educational orientations leads to a critical crossroads in field practice. By examining these differences, we aim to understand how they can complement rather than conflict with each other, forging a path forward that is as comprehensive as it is empathetic.

Anti-Oppression and Psychoanalysis

The chasm between anti-oppressive and psychoanalytic theories in psychotherapy is vast and complex, yet both seek the common ground of client well-being. Anti-oppressive theory serves as the vanguard for addressing power dynamics, privilege, and systemic inequalities. It fosters an acute awareness of societal structures—racism, sexism, and other forms of oppression—and their insidious impact on an individual's mental health. The primary goal is to cultivate a therapeutic milieu that is inclusive and validating, a haven where clients can unpack their experiences within these oppressive systems without fear of marginalization.

Psychoanalytic theory, with its genesis in the work of Freud, dives into the murky waters of the unconscious, childhood experiences, and the intricate dance of client-therapist dynamics. Its pursuit is to bring to light the unconscious conflicts and unresolved issues from our earliest narratives that haunt the present. This exploration is not merely an academic pursuit; it seeks to engender insight, foster personal growth, and facilitate healing through an understanding of unconscious motivations and past experiences.

While they diverge in focus, both approaches possess unique strengths that can be harnessed in the service of therapeutic work. Anti-oppression theory provides a lens with which to view the individual within a broader societal context, acknowledging the weight of systemic influences on mental health. Psychoanalytic theory offers a deep dive into personal history, revealing patterns that shape current functioning. The modern therapist often finds merit in integrating these theories, weaving together a comprehensive approach that honours the individual's story within the tapestry of societal constructs.

The integration of anti-oppressive theory into psychotherapy calls for a recognition of intersectionality and cultural competence, as discussed by Timothy & Umana Garcia (2020) and Tummala-Narra et al. (2018). These authors highlight the importance of considering the multiple, intersecting identities of clients and how these facets of identity contribute to experiences of oppression and psychological distress.

In practice, this integration is less a matter of blending colors on a palette and more akin to orchestrating a symphony, with each theory contributing its own timbre and tone to the collective harmony of client care. The next section will detail how an anti-oppression-informed approach can be manifested in psychotherapy, followed by an exposition of contemporary psychoanalytic psychotherapy.

Anti-oppression-informed Psychotherapy

Anti-oppression-informed psychotherapy is an approach that aims to address the power imbalances and systemic injustices that can impact a person's mental health and well-being. It recognizes that various forms of oppression, such as racism, sexism, homophobia, ableism and more can contribute to psychological distress. The goal of anti-oppressive psychotherapy is to create a therapeutic environment that empowers individuals to explore and challenge these societal dynamics while promoting their agency, resilience, and overall mental health.

Key Features and Methods

1. Cultural Sensitivity: Therapists practicing anti-oppressive psychotherapy are trained to be culturally sensitive and aware of the diverse backgrounds, experiences and identities of their clients. This includes understanding the impact of culture and systemic biases on mental health.

2. Intersectionality: This approach recognizes that individuals hold multiple identities and that their experiences of oppression are interconnected. For example, a Black, queer woman might face unique challenges at the intersections of race, gender, and sexual orientation. Therapists consider these intersections when working with clients.

3. Power Dynamics: Anti-oppressive psychotherapy seeks to equalize power dynamics between therapist and client. Therapists aim to be collaborative, fostering a safe space where clients can voice their concerns without fear of judgment or re-traumatization.

4. Critical Analysis: Clients are encouraged to critically analyse their experiences and consider how societal structures contribute to their mental health struggles. This involves exploring how oppression, discrimination and marginalization impact their self-perception and life choices.

The cultural sensitivity and awareness of systemic biases in mental health are crucial components of anti-oppressive psychotherapy. Yee & Wagner (2013) argue that anti-oppression teaching, while vital, can inadvertently perpetuate neo-liberal ideals if not critically examined. Their work prompts a re-evaluation of how anti-oppressive principles are taught and applied, ensuring they truly serve the interests of clients and communities.

The therapeutic practice includes addressing internalized negative beliefs and celebrating the client's self-identification, advocating for their autonomy in defining their own existence. In practice, anti-oppression-informed psychotherapy does not merely apply a set of techniques; it embodies a philosophy of care that is as much about healing as it is about empowerment and advocacy. This commitment to addressing the broader societal context within individual therapy sessions sets the stage for a more expansive and equitable form of mental health care.

Case Study - Racial Identity and Trauma

Consider a client, Maya, a young African American woman grappling with the aftermath of racial profiling and discrimination. In sessions, her therapist does not merely listen; they actively engage with Maya's narrative, validating her lived experiences while helping her to dissect the insidious effects of systemic racism on her psyche. Maya speaks of walking through stores and feeling the weight of surveillance, the unwarranted scrutiny that she internalizes as a reflection of her worth. The therapist guides Maya through the process of acknowledging her trauma, fostering a sense of empowerment by affirming her right to dignity and respect. Together, they explore strategies for resilience, such as strengthening community connections and engaging in social activism, which serve as therapeutic counterpoints to the isolation and self-doubt inflicted by racism.

Case Study - Gender and Sexuality

In another therapeutic alliance, Alex, a non-binary individual, confronts the challenges of existing outside binary gender norms in a society that often rejects such fluidity. Alex's therapist employs an anti-oppressive approach to help them navigate the intricate layers of their identity, from the anxiety of public perception to the complexities of intimate relationships. The therapist provides a space for Alex to voice their fears of rejection and identify instances of microaggressions, all while reinforcing their journey towards self-acceptance. This work extends beyond the individual, as the therapist encourages Alex to explore the broader LGBTQ+ community, fostering connections that reinforce their sense of belonging and identity. The therapeutic work includes addressing internalized negative beliefs and celebrating the client's self-identification, advocating for their autonomy in defining their own existence.

In practice, anti-oppression-informed psychotherapy does not merely apply a set of techniques; it embodies a philosophy of care that is as much about healing as it is about empowerment and advocacy. This commitment to addressing the broader societal context within individual therapy sessions sets the stage for a more expansive and equitable form of mental health care.

Contemporary psychoanalytic psychotherapy

Contemporary psychoanalytic psychotherapy is a therapeutic approach rooted in Sigmund Freud's original psychoanalytic theories but adapted to modern contexts. It focuses on exploring the unconscious mind, childhood experiences and the dynamics of interpersonal relationships to understand and address psychological challenges. This therapy typically involves weekly sessions where the client talks about their thoughts, feelings, dreams and memories while the therapist listens attentively and interprets underlying patterns.

Shedler (2022) asserts that contemporary psychoanalytic psychotherapy remains a vibrant and essential modality, adapting Freud's foundational principles to the complexities of modern mental health issues. He emphasizes the continued relevance of exploring the unconscious and interpersonal dynamics as a pathway to understanding and healing: "[Psychodynamic therapy] is not about archaic theories or historical curiosities. It is about understanding the mind and the human condition in ways that are timeless and universally applicable (p. 5)." Shedler further clarifies, "Contemporary psychoanalytic therapy involves 'working with emotion in the here and now, exploring attempts to avoid painful thoughts and feelings, identifying recurring themes and patterns in patients' lives, discussing past experience in the light of present knowledge, and focusing on patients' relationships and interpersonal experience (p. 9)."

Contemporary psychoanalytic psychotherapy is used to (according to McWilliams - Replay, 2021):

» Explore unconscious patterns: It helps individuals identify and address underlying emotions and motivations that influence their thoughts and behaviors.

» Enhance self-awareness: Clients gain insights into their inner world, improving their understanding of how past experiences shape their present challenges.

» Improve relationships: By uncovering relationship patterns and attachment styles, clients can work on improving their interactions with others.

» Alleviate symptoms: Understanding the root causes of psychological distress can lead to symptom relief and long-term emotional well-being.

Case Study - Attachment

Sarah, a client who presents with anxiety and a history of challenging relationships, begins her therapeutic journey with an exploration of her attachment style, which appears to be anxiously preoccupied. Week by week, she and her therapist peel back the layers of her past, discovering a recurring theme of emotional neglect. It becomes clear that Sarah's adult relationships are haunted by the spectre of her childhood, where she often felt unseen and unheard. This revelation brings forth a profound empathy for her younger self, and, with the guidance of her therapist, Sarah begins to forge a new narrative—one in which she can seek out and maintain secure, nurturing relationships without the paralyzing fear of abandonment.

Case Study - Depression

John enters therapy feeling weighed down by a cloak of depression and a pervasive sense of unworthiness. As he explores the terrain of his past with his therapist, they uncover a pattern of critical and dismissive messages from a parent during his formative years, messages that John internalized and which now form the bedrock of his low self-esteem. In the safety of the therapeutic space, John confronts these repressed feelings of inadequacy. His therapist, acting as both witness and guide, helps John to challenge these ingrained beliefs and to cultivate a compassionate self-regard. Through this psychodynamic work, John gradually reconstructs his self-image from one marred by criticism to one that acknowledges and celebrates his intrinsic value.

Tensions in Anti-Oppressive and Psychoanalytic Theories

The therapeutic neutrality of psychoanalysis can sometimes seem at odds with the advocacy inherent in anti-oppressive practice. Aibel (2017) examines the political dimensions within the consulting room and how these can influence the therapeutic process. He notes that "the personal is political is psychoanalytic," highlighting how politics can permeate the consulting room and shape the dynamics between therapist and client. This complex interplay can add a layer of depth to the therapeutic process, though it also introduces challenges in maintaining the analytic space.

Schamess (2006) further explores this tension by examining transference enactments in clinical supervision, providing insight into how unconscious dynamics between therapist and client can manifest and influence the supervisory relationship. He emphasizes the importance of recognizing these enactments as opportunities to understand and work through underlying conflicts and resistances, stating that "transference enactments in clinical supervision can reveal as much about the supervisee's internal world as they do about the client's psychological state."

As a clinical supervisor, one encounters a myriad of theoretical crosscurrents that supervisees must navigate. Here, I outline six tensions that frequently emerge when supervisees adhere strictly to an anti-oppressive framework, often at the expense of psychoanalytic insights.

Tensions in Anti-Oppressive (AO) and Psychoanalytic (PA) Theories

1	AO	Ongoing considerations for increasing accessibility, particularly for marginalized populations
	PA	Maintaining the therapeutic frame and analysing the impact of modifying the frame
2	AO	An emphasis on what the client brings in at face value; more goal-directed and client-driven work with hesitation to collect in-depth history
	PA	Developing a curiosity based on comprehensive history taking; ability to challenge or counter what client articulates
3	AO	Inclinations toward client advocacy and perhaps becoming solution-focused
	PA	Interrogation of the therapist's desire to deviate from the frame; exploring countertransference
4	AO	Understanding ruptures through self-reflexivity and exploration of the therapist's power and social location
	PA	Understanding ruptures as an enactment, unconscious role response, or projective identification—all of which originate from the client
5	AO	Effective use-of-self, intended to normalize client experience, lateralize power or communicate cultural safety
	PA	Endeavour to suspend personal disclosure in order to further explore transference
6	AO	Abrupt termination: Self-determination, readiness for therapy
	PA	Abrupt termination: Possible enactments resulting from the unconscious of both therapist and client

Accessibility vs. Therapeutic Frame

The anti-oppressive approach vigorously advocates for increased accessibility, especially for marginalized populations, often challenging traditional therapeutic frameworks. This contrasts with the psychodynamic emphasis on maintaining the therapeutic frame, which is seen as essential to the analytic process. The tension arises in balancing the need to adapt therapy to be more inclusive, without diluting the structure that gives psychoanalysis its therapeutic potency.

The push for accessibility in anti-oppressive practice often involves questioning and modifying the traditional therapeutic setting to accommodate diverse client needs. This can include flexible scheduling, sliding scale fees, and creating a physically and emotionally safe space for marginalized clients (Timothy & Umana Garcia, 2020). However, from a psychodynamic perspective, altering the therapeutic frame, such as the consistency of sessions and the physical setup of the therapy room, can impact the containment and boundary-setting essential for analytic work (Gray, 2013). Balancing these needs requires a nuanced understanding of how changes in the frame can both advance and hinder therapeutic progress.

Client's Presenting Concerns vs. In-Depth History

Anti-oppressive therapy values the client's presenting concerns and directs therapy towards immediate, goal-oriented work. Psychodynamic therapy, in contrast, delves into an in-depth historical analysis, positing that a comprehensive understanding of the client's past is essential to address current issues. The tension here is in valuing what the client brings to the session, while also fostering a curiosity that extends beyond the present to historical roots.

In anti-oppressive therapy, immediate concerns are prioritized to address pressing issues and empower the client. This approach aligns with the ethos of being client-driven and valuing the lived experiences and narratives that clients bring into the therapy room (Lee & Rasmussen, 2019). Conversely, the psychodynamic approach emphasizes the importance of a thorough historical analysis, believing that past experiences significantly shape current behavior and experiences (Bateman, Holmes, & Allison, 2022). The challenge lies in integrating the immediate, present-focused approach of anti-oppressive therapy with the depth and richness of a historical exploration typical of psychodynamic therapy.

Advocacy vs. Analytic Neutrality

An anti-oppressive stance often leads to a natural inclination towards advocacy and solution-focused interventions. However, this orientation can be at odds with the psychodynamic approach, which involves examining the therapist's impulses to act—often conceptualized as countertransference—and maintaining a degree of neutrality to preserve the analytic space. The challenge lies in supporting the client's empowerment without foreclosing the exploration of unconscious dynamics.

Advocacy is a cornerstone of anti-oppressive practice, wherein therapists actively work to validate and support clients' experiences of oppression and work towards societal change (Agass, 2002). This can sometimes contrast with the psychodynamic principle of analytic neutrality, where therapists are encouraged to maintain a neutral, reflective stance to facilitate the exploration of the client's unconscious processes (Goren, 2013). Striking a balance between these positions involves recognizing when to employ advocacy to support the client while preserving the reflective space necessary for deep analytic work.

Ruptures in Therapy

From an anti-oppressive perspective, ruptures in the therapeutic relationship are often examined through the lens of the therapist's power and social location, emphasizing self-reflexivity. Psychoanalysis is more likely to interpret ruptures as enactments or projective identifications that originate from the client's unconscious. The tension lies in understanding these ruptures as both a reflection of the client's inner world and a manifestation of the relational dynamics, including the therapist's own contributions.

Anti-oppressive therapy views ruptures as opportunities to explore power dynamics and the therapist's contributions to the therapeutic relationship (Washington, Williams, & Byrd, 2023). Psychoanalysis, however, often interprets ruptures as manifestations of the client's unconscious conflicts (Schamess, 2006). Understanding these ruptures requires a framework that acknowledges the validity of both perspectives, seeing ruptures as both a reflection of the client's inner world and the dynamics of the therapeutic relationship, including systemic and individual factors.

Use of Self in Therapy

Anti-oppressive therapy encourages therapists to use self-disclosure as a means to normalize the client's experience and lateralize power dynamics. On the other hand, psychoanalysis traditionally endeavours to limit therapist self-disclosure to further explore transference. The tension is in determining when and how therapist self-disclosure can be therapeutic without detracting from the client's transference exploration.

The use of self-disclosure in anti-oppressive therapy is seen as a way to build authenticity and trust, particularly when working with clients from marginalized backgrounds (MacKenzie, 2023). Psychoanalysis traditionally values the therapist's anonymity to facilitate transference analysis (Aibel, 2017). Navigating this tension involves discerning when self-disclosure serves the therapeutic process and when it might hinder the exploration of transference and countertransference dynamics.

Termination of Therapy

The anti-oppressive approach respects the client's self-determination and readiness for therapy, which can sometimes lead to abrupt terminations. In contrast, psychoanalysis views abrupt terminations as possible enactments from the unconscious processes of both therapist and client, suggesting a deeper exploration. The tension is in respecting client autonomy while being mindful of the potential unconscious dynamics at play.

Respecting the client's readiness for therapy and self-determination is central to anti-oppressive practice, which may lead to abrupt or client-initiated terminations (Timothy & Umana Garcia, 2020). Psychoanalytic theory, however, suggests exploring the unconscious meanings and motivations behind abrupt terminations, viewing them as potential enactments or resistances (Zetzer et al., 2020). Therapists must be attuned to the balance between honouring client autonomy and exploring the unconscious dynamics that may be influencing the decision to terminate.

Conclusion

This paper embarked on a nuanced exploration of the intersection between anti-oppressive perspectives and psychodynamic theory, particularly within the realm of clinical supervision. Through the detailed dissection of six inherent tensions, we've illuminated the intricate dance between accommodating the pressing needs of the present, as rooted in anti-oppressive practice, and delving into the depths of the unconscious, as emphasized in psychoanalytic theory.

In their examination of counsellor supervision models, Washington et al. (2023) identify blind spots and hidden curricula that may influence the integration of therapeutic perspectives. They highlight the importance of supervisors being aware of these implicit biases and structures to facilitate a more effective and integrated approach to therapy.

The journey through these tensions underscores the importance of not merely recognizing but embracing the complexity of integrating these modalities. It calls for a supervision framework that is not only adaptive and reflective but also critically aware and psychodynamically informed. The goal is to forge a therapeutic practice that is as socially conscious as it is individually attuned, recognizing that the path to healing is as much about navigating the social landscapes as it is about exploring the personal narratives.

In light of this exploration, I propose several future directions:

1. Development of supervision models that explicitly address the integration of anti-oppressive and psychoanalytic perspectives, offering practical guidelines for navigating the outlined tensions.

2. Further research into the outcomes of such integrated practices, focusing on client experiences and therapeutic effectiveness.

3. Training programs for supervisors and therapists that emphasize the development of skills in both anti-oppressive practice and psychoanalytic theory, fostering a generation of practitioners adept in navigating the complexities of modern psychotherapy.

Therefore, the integration of anti-oppressive perspectives and psychodynamic theory in clinical supervision is not merely an academic endeavour; it is a commitment to a more holistic, empathetic, and effective practice of psychotherapy. It is about honouring the diverse narratives of our clients and recognizing that the journey to healing is multifaceted, requiring a therapeutic approach that is as rich and varied as the human experience itself.

References

Agass, D. (2002). Countertransference, supervision and the reflection process. *Journal of Social Work Practice,* 16(2), 125–133. https://doi.org/10.1080/0265053022000033694

Aibel, M. (2017). The Personal is political is psychoanalytic: Politics in the consulting room. *Psychoanalytic Perspectives,* 15(1), 64–101. https://doi.org/10.1080/1551806x.2018.1396130

Avilés-Acosta, J., Das, A., Santiago, J., Rivera, J., & Torres Fernández, I. (n.d.). Applying liberation psychology for an anti-hegemonic supervision praxis. [In Press].

Bateman, A., Holmes, J., & Allison, E. (2022). *Introduction to psychoanalysis: contemporary theory and practice.* London; New York Routledge, Taylor Et Francis.

Goren, E. (2013). Ethics, boundaries, and supervision. Commentary on trauma triangles and parallel processes: Geometry and the supervisor/trainee/patient triad. *Psychoanalytic Dialogues,* 23(6), 737–743. https://doi.org/10.1080/10481885.2013.851568

Gray, A. (2013). *An Introduction to the Therapeutic Frame.* Routledge.

Hall, J. C. (2018). Black women talk about stereotypical transference enactments in cross-cultural supervision. *Journal of Human Behavior in the Social Environment,* 28(8), 1019–1032. https://doi.org/10.1080/10911359.2018.1489930

Hall, J. C., & Spencer, R. E. (2017). Illuminating the phenomenological challenges of cross-cultural supervision. *Smith College Studies in Social Work,* 87(2-3), 238–253. https://doi.org/10.1080/00377317.2017.1324108

Lee, E., & Rasmussen, B. (2019). Psychoanalysis, socioanalysis, and social work: Psychodynamic contributions to understanding diversity, power, and institutions in social work practice. *Smith College Studies in Social Work,* 89(2), 83–90. https://doi.org/10.1080/00377317.2019.1686873

MacKenzie, Lily G., (2023). "Is that my agenda or is that serving the client?": Perspectives of social justice-oriented counsellors on working with clients who express oppressive views." *Electronic Thesis and Dissertation Repository.* 9190. https://ir.lib.uwo.ca/etd/9190

Mills, J. (2005). A critique of relational psychoanalysis. *Psychoanalytic Psychology,* 22(2), 155–188. https://doi.org/10.1037/0736-9735.22.2.155

Schamess, G. (2006). Transference enactments in clinical supervision. *Clinical Social Work Journal,* 34(4), 407–425. https://doi.org/10.1007/s10615-005-0036-y

Shedler, J. (2022). That was then, this is now: Psychoanalytic psychotherapy for the rest of us. *Contemporary Psychoanalysis,* 58(2-3), 405–437. https://doi.org/10.1080/00107530.2022.2149038

Stevenson, S. (2019). A racist attack managing complex relationships with traumatised service users – a psychodynamic approach. *Journal of Social Work Practice,* 34(3), 225–235. https://doi.org/10.1080/02650533.2019.1648247

Susanne Bennett, C. (2008). The interface of attachment, transference, and countertransference: Implications for the clinical supervisory relationship. *Smith College Studies in Social Work,* 78(2-3), 301–320. https://doi.org/10.1080/00377310802114635

Thyer, B. A. (2015). It is time to delink psychodynamic theory from the definition of clinical social work. *Clinical Social Work Journal,* 45(4), 364–366. https://doi.org/10.1007/s10615-015-0530-9

Timothy, R. K., & Umana Garcia, M. (2020). Anti-oppression psychotherapy: An emancipatory integration of intersectionality into psychotherapy. *Psychotherapy and Counselling Journal of Australia,* 8(2). https://doi.org/10.59158/001c.71085

Tummala-Narra, P. (2015). Cultural competence as a core emphasis of psychoanalytic psychotherapy. *Psychoanalytic Psychology,* 32(2), 275–292. https://doi.org/10.1037/a0034041

Tummala-Narra, P., Claudius, M., Letendre, P. J., Sarbu, E., Teran, V., & Villalba, W. (2018). Psychoanalytic psychologists' conceptualizations of cultural competence in psychotherapy. *Psychoanalytic Psychology,* 35(1), 46–59. https://doi.org/10.1037/pap0000150

Washington, A. R., Williams, J. M., & Byrd, J. A. (2023). Exposing blindspots and the hidden curriculum within counselor supervision models. *Counselor Education and Supervision,* 62(2), 149–156. https://doi.org/10.1002/ceas.12260

What Actually Heals in Therapy with Psychoanalyst Nancy McWilliams - Replay. (2021, September 15). *Therapist Uncensored.* https://therapistuncensored.com/episodes/tu156-what-actually-heals-in-therapy-with-psychoanalyst-nancy-mcwilliams-replay/

Yee, J. Y., & Wagner, A. E. (2013). Is anti-oppression teaching in Canadian social work classrooms a form of Neo-Liberalism? *Social Work Education,* 32(3), 331–348. https://doi.org/10.1080/02615479.2012.672557

Ying Yee, J., & Wagner, A. (2013). Intercultural therapy. *Social Work Education,* 32(3), 331–348. https://doi.org/10.1080/02615479.2012.672557

Zetzer, H. A., Hill, C. E., Hopsicker, R. J., Krasno, A. M., Montojo, P. C., Plumb, E. I. W., Hoffman, M. A., & Donahue, M. T. (2020). Parallel process in psychodynamic supervision: The supervisor's perspective. *Psychotherapy,* 57(2), 252–262. https://doi.org/10.1037/pst0000274

Bathhouse Counselling, Or the Relevance of Psychoanalytic Interventions In Clinical Social Work

MARCO POSADAS, PHD, RSW

This article explores ways in which psychoanalytic theory and technique can help clinical social workers and psychoanalytic clinicians face some of the challenges of working with difficult-to-access populations. It addresses how to bridge gaps in mental health services by doing culturally sensitive mental health outreach to specific vulnerable communities. The article addresses clinical competencies, and how we can strengthen them with psychoanalytic theory to reach out to marginalized populations considered difficult to reach (Berzoff, Flanagan, & Hertz, 2016, pp. 1-17). Specifically, this article examines the experience of providing mental health counseling in male bathhouses, using psychoanalytic theory to support a single session counseling model geared toward decreasing the risk of HIV transmissions among gay, bisexual, and other men who have sex with men (MSM; AIDS Committee of Toronto, 2011). I use a bathhouse counseling program as an example of community-based clinical social work that benefited from psychoanalytic theory to support my argument. I argue that psychoanalysis is particularly useful to strengthen community-based interventions by expanding our understanding of the unconscious instinctual conflicts that come into play for our most marginalized clients (Berzoff et al., 2016). In the same way, psychoanalysis as a body of knowledge has benefited from clinical social work, critical race theory, queer theory, transgender studies, prejudice studies, etc. I personally have always wanted to make psychoanalysis accessible to marginalized populations. I have seen how psychoanalytic theory can strengthen the social worker's skills; it can inform successful mental health interventions by providing depth to our case formulations, and provide a practical clinical way to do anti-oppressive clinical interventions.

An example would be the way in which the psychoanalytic social worker uses neutrality in the clinical setting. I mean neutrality not as the misrepresentation of classical Freudian technique (Freud, 1912b, 1913, 1919), but as the complex set of skills and interventions in the therapeutic dyad that prevents the clinician from othering the client and allowing the therapeutic action to move forward.

My interest in this type of clinical work comes from my journey to become a psychoanalytic clinician and the barriers I have experienced along the way as I tried to access this type of training in Mexico City. I have been immersed in cultures where stigma toward accessing mental health services is unfamiliar and prejudice against psychoanalysis is not mainstream, nor reflected in the way mental health clinicians are trained. For instance, in Mexico and other Latin American cultures, psychoanalysis is regarded as one of the most useful forms of mental health treatment (Gallo, 2010). This particular prevalence of psychoanalytic thinking in Mexico is understood as influenced by the individual's need to effectively change their circumstances, and external difficulties to impact their external world. Thus the person can draw upon a frustration with the external world as a motivation to create psychic change (Ramirez, 1978). Psychoanalysis helps the person deal with the difficulty of systemic oppression embedded in political and social systems at an individual level (Bolognini, 2011). Even words associated with psychoanalysis, such as some diagnostic labels like hysteria, and defense mechanisms such as projection or denial are part of pop culture.

In places like Buenos Aires, Argentina, the Argentine Psychoanalytic Association (APA) accounts for almost 10% of the International Psychoanalytical Association (IPA); APA is one of three IPA-affiliated institutes in Buenos Aires alone. Out of 14,000 IPA members around the world, 1,200 are in APA, and in Brazil alone the Brazilian Association of Candidates harbors more than 900 psychoanalysts-to-be out of 4,000 internationally. During my first psychoanalytic conference in Buenos Aires, I spent my ride listening to the cab driver's experience of thrice-weekly analysis on the couch: "Who has the time to do five?!" He was able to articulate how analysis benefited him after his wife left him and moved to a different city four hours away from Buenos Aires, taking their two children with her: "Psychoanalysis helped me survive that loss."

Finally, in some communities across Latin America, access to psychotherapy can be seen as a privilege that may lead toward class acceptance and class privilege. It was only when I moved to North America that I experienced first-hand the prejudice toward psychoanalysis, and the stigma against accessing mental health as mainstream and normative. But why is this important to social workers?

Psychoanalysis and clinical social work

We have to acknowledge that psychoanalysis has been pushed to the margins of the mental health discourse in private and public institutions (Goldstein, 2009). Some of this marginalization may be in part a reflection of how poorly psychoanalysis has collaborated with other mental health professions. Organized psychoanalysis has been pushed outside of health care and academic institutions as a result of a history of not being inclusive with other professions outside of medicine (Loewenberg & Thompson, 2011). In academic institutions, it is a recurrent conversation within the IPA how psychoanalytic academic programs are decreasing in the United States and Canada. Cultural biases embedded in Freud's Victorian-era thinking were reflected in the choice of language and the theory itself. Unfortunate concepts such as "penis envy" (Freud, 1908), "the vagina dentata" (Freud, 1905), and "women as the dark continent... with more relaxed superegos" (Freud, 1925 p.244) are classic academic examples of misogyny embedded in Freudian concepts that inform the stereotype of the prejudiced psychoanalyst.

Freud's papers on female sexuality (1925, 1931, 1933) are the poster child for academics that use Freud's culturally normative prejudice to dismiss psychoanalytic clinical concepts such as neutrality, transference, and countertransference. It is well-known how in psychiatry in general and psychotherapy in particular there is a push toward medication and brief interventions. In psychology, a push toward standardization is only one in a lineup of arguments against psychoanalysis, and followed by their unfair rejection from training institutes in the early days of the psychoanalytic movement in the United States. This type of professional rejection from psychoanalytic institutions may have fueled psychologists to develop cognitive behavioral therapy (CBT) as a response (Loewenberg & Thompson, 2011).

In social work, too, we have a complicated relationship between psychoanalysis and clinical social work practice. We can have different and contradictory arguments that result in what I see as an erasure of psychoanalytic thinking from clinical social work practice. Similar to psychologists, social workers were excluded from organized psychoanalytic training (Perlman, 1994). Stigmatized as only useful to "worried well" (Specht & Courtney, 1994, in Goldstein, 2009), psychoanalysis has been dismissed and erased from the foundations of the clinical aspects of our profession.

An accurate representation of the complicated relationship between psychoanalysis and social work can be the case of Bertha Pappenheim, Freud's famous Anna O. It is well-documented that Pappenheim was not pleased with the outcome of her treatment with Freud. She became one of the first social workers and feminists of her time in Germany right after she discontinued analysis with Freud (Swenson, 1994). I wonder if we, social workers, unconsciously inherited that conflict and bear it in our identity as social workers and psychoanalysts (Goldstein, 2009).

Another example of this type of unconscious erasure of psychoanalysis from our thinking as social workers can be seen in Sakamoto and Pitner (2005). Some of their arguments and recommendations presented about anti-oppressive practice could be supported by psychoanalytic theory, but instead they stop with Freire (1970). They argue the importance of "critical consciousness" to anti-oppressive practice, and offer it as a tool to understand and deconstruct power dynamics at a personal level, without really acknowledging psychoanalytic contributions that support Freire's work. The authors refer to the origin of the concept of "critical consciousness" and connect it to Freire without accounting for Fromm's and Freud's influence in Freire's work (Freire, 1970).

The connection of Freire's work to psychoanalysis has been discussed before in papers outside of social work (Bingham, 2002), and it is well-known in Latin America. Here is where I see how important it is for psychoanalytic social workers to develop and expand current knowledge of the intersection between psychoanalysis and anti-oppressive practice. This will inevitably strengthen our work as clinical social workers. I use TowelTalk as an example that shows psychoanalytically informed anti-oppressive practice, and how these types of interventions can support the provision of mental health services in community spaces that are believed to be non-conducive for counseling (Berzoff et al., 2016; Cattaneo et al., 2009).

Context

In the past 60 years, psychoanalysis has been criticized as an inadequate scientific clinical intervention for diverse communities in North America (Aron, Lews, & Starr, 2013; Akhtar, 2014; Berzoff et al., 2016; Herzog, 2015; Roughton, 2002). During this time, psychoanalysis has lost important clinical spaces to what are believed to be more "evidence-based," "short-term," "cost-effective," and "strengths-based" approaches. As I mentioned earlier, psychoanalysis can be perceived as threatening to the status quo, and a complicated theory in realms like social work, psychology, and psychiatry—inside and outside academic contexts. At the same time, we continue to hear in psychoanalytic conferences about an emphasis in showcasing psychoanalytic research, and developing research agendas that can translate to larger audiences how psychoanalytic treatment works (Altmann, Fitzpatrick-Hanly, & Leuzinger-Bohleber, 2012; Lemma, Target, & Fonagy, 2010; Leuzinger-Bohleber, 2004; Malberg, Fonagy, & Mayes, 2008).

Accordingly, important community-based interventions supported in rigorous research have been consistently appearing in Europe, the United States, and Latin America. We have heard about different approaches to deliver psychoanalytically informed interventions that reach diverse communities and tackle complex research questions that support psychoanalysis as a valuable evidence-based intervention (Busch, Milrod, & Sandberg, 2009; Leuzinger-Bohleber, Stuhrast, R€uger, & Beutel, 2003; Panel, 2008). These programs are bringing together allies and building bridges to respond to the challenge to make psychoanalytically informed interventions accessible for populations that would otherwise be deemed not appropriate for psychoanalytic treatment.

In a way, we can say that we have been thinking outside of the couch, but the reality is that we have been working hard through decades of successful interventions and building upon our clinical traditions. And we are not even touching on the political and financial aspects of prioritizing one form of mental health intervention over another.

As I researched articles and spoke to senior clinicians, supervisors, and peers, I realized that part of the work that I do, although it is a unique and innovative community-based intervention, stands upon foundations shaped by clinicians before me. These clinicians faced the same challenges of identifying missed opportunities and dealt with the apparent paradox of reconciling what is different within psychoanalysis. My work follows a line of psychoanalytic clinicians and clinical social workers who forged new territories for practice and training.

I will use Winnicott's concept of "holding environment" (Winnicott, 1945, 1986), specifically referring to the maternal/parent function of holding the fragmented and disavowed aspects of the child. I will apply such concepts from an anti-oppressive perspective to mental health services (Freire, 1970; Mullaly, 2002; Sakamoto & Pitner, 2005; Williams, 2002). My hope is to contribute to the already existing dialogue between psychoanalysis and anti-oppressive clinical practice (e.g., Davids, 2003; Kantor, in press; Leary, 2007; Rasmussen & Salhani, 2010; Suchet, 2007) and highlight the relevance that psychoanalytic thought has to increase the competency of clinical social workers to address the mental health needs of gay, bisexual, and other MSM who would otherwise get lost in our system.

In this article, I share the way in which the clinician can carve a space to think within a highly sexualized environment to reach those who have fallen through the cracks of our mental health care system, and some lessons learned from that experience. These are attempts to bring psychoanalytic understanding to community- based clinical social work, and my way of doing psychoanalytic outreach; to support community-based interventions with psychoanalytic thinking to benefit diverse marginalized communities, and to further the realm of applied psychoanalysis within clinical social work. Furthermore, by developing psychoanalytic-informed interventions in a nontraditional setting, I was able to find a creative compromise to resolve the tension of being a psychoanalytic clinical social worker.

Let's face it: psychoanalysis has consistently struggled with diversities in general and difference in particular (Bernardi, 1992; Freud, 1925, 1931, 1933; Glocer Fiorini, 2017; Stone, 1954). Although culturally appropriate at the time, this inherited intolerance to difference was bound to cause tension in the identity of the clinical social worker and the importance of addressing social justice as one of our professional values. I believe this tension forces the psychoanalytic social worker to adhere firmly to theory in an attempt to resolve it. This inadvertently increases the tension by approaching theory dogmatically.

In my experience, ideas of what psychoanalysis is supposed to be (Stone, 1954) usually adhere to psychoanalysis as a pure craft, and anything different is rejected as wild psychoanalysis (Bernardi, 1992; Stone, 1954). Rigid ideas about psychoanalysis get compounded with socially sanctioned prejudices that analytic candidates and trainees internalize via their own training. These unconscious prejudices later become part of the analytic identity of the clinician and can operate as bastions in the mind of the social worker, and mobilize them to participate in an enactment (Baranger & Baranger, 2008; Cassorla, 2005; Ravitz & Maunder, 2015). But why do a therapeutic counseling program in a bathhouse?

Program description

TowelTalk is a bathhouse counseling program in Toronto geared to providing psychosocial support for men who are at risk of contracting

HIV and other sexually transmitted infections (STIs). Bathhouses are licensed commercial venues where, historically, gay, bisexual, and other MSM gather to connect with other men in various ways. In Toronto, these are places where a man can access a space to have sex, relax, exercise, watch pornography, lounge, and listen to music while remaining anonymous. Although bathhouses have been the cornerstone for HIV prevention campaigns since the late 1980s (AIDS Committee of Toronto, 2011), they are spaces where HIV transmission still persists. Bathhouses are commonly associated with words such as "danger," "risk," "sordid," "gross," "dark," "dirty," and "bad" by people familiar and unfamiliar with these facilities. Both patrons and service providers (bathhouses in Toronto are frequented by AIDS Service Organizations, and other community agencies to provide sexual health outreach, HIV and STI testing, and recently mental health counseling) alike experience these sites as anxiety provoking and complicated spaces, while also finding them intriguing and fun. Bathhouses institutionalize anonymity and provide an alternative option to establish contact between MSM. Anonymity thus protects and empowers some bathhouse patrons, generating a sense of "apparent safety" where men can explore and try new or different behaviors.

As a result, these spaces can attract diverse populations of men who can benefit from such anonymity and safety: young men, men from racialized communities, newcomers to Canada, men who are under-housed or with complicated housing arrangements, men who use substances, men who are married to women, men who are at risk of contracting HIV, and men who are affected by or living with HIV (AIDS Committee of Toronto, 2011). I have to make an important distinction: "feeling safe in anonymity" does not mean free of anxiety and affects, whether conscious or unconscious (Fernando, 2009; Freud, 1926; Rapaport, 1953).

Imagine this scene as the setting: The typical bathhouse is a mix between a gym and a nightclub with a locker room area, and includes benches, mirrors, water fountains, weights and treadmills. It is like a nightclub with a DJ booth but no dance floor. There are whirlpools that fit 10 to 12 men each, lounge areas with several flat-screen TVs on and showing mostly gay pornography; dry and steam saunas with showers; and dark rooms with military motifs and built-in structures creating mazes. Small openings in the walls of these mazes, known as "glory holes," can enhance the anonymity of an encounter by allowing for exposure of only a part of one's body (usually the genitals) to another patron on the other side of the wall. Low-lit and air-conditioned rooms in different sizes are available for rent, laid out to create halls and pathways for men to walk around and cruise. Depending on the size of the room, they have beds, slings, mirrors, TVs, and metallic fixtures that give them an industrial feeling. In addition to this, it is mandatory for patrons to wear only a towel while they stay in the bathhouse. With this image in mind, we can more easily picture the highly sexualized environment characteristic of bathhouses, which bathhouse counselors are exposed to.

TowelTalk is a free counseling program that places professional counselors in four of Toronto's male bathhouses. It is funded by the Ontario Ministry of Health and Long-Term Care, AIDS Bureau, and is part of the AIDS Committee of Toronto (ACT). In its origin it was supported by a Program Advisory Committee, which included community partners, a clinical consultant, and a program supervisor who managed the three bathhouse counselors who continue to be responsible for program coordination and service provision. TowelTalk has a program evaluation component, and a research subcommittee initially evaluated the feasibility of the program by formative and process structures (AIDS Committee of Toronto, 2011). This committee currently evaluates patrons' satisfaction with the program, and is working on a qualitative study of the experiences of the counselors providing this intervention.

TowelTalk counselors attend bathhouses, fully clothed, to offer single-session therapeutic counseling on a walk-in basis to bathhouse patrons with the objective of reducing the risk of HIV transmission. Each counselor provides three-hour shifts in one of the rooms described earlier, made available by the bathhouse management. At an agency level, TowelTalk aims to increase access to psychosocial support to enhance sexual health and the emotional and psychological well-being of gay, bisexual, and other MSM. It has been our experience that sessions usually start by bathhouse patrons "hitting on" the counselor, and propositioning him for sex. The counselor politely turns down any sexual proposition and uses this to engage with the patron in a conversation that might provide hints of openings for a counseling session. Openings are opportunities for the counselor to tap into the patron's material; they then flag the possibility of a TowelTalk session. Outreach workers and HIV and STI testers are trained to stay away from "difficult themes," what I call openings. Not every patron will provide openings on their initial interaction with the counselor, as most of the patrons might not feel the need to talk to someone. This sometimes sparks the patron's curiosity, as the idea of counseling in bathhouses is rather new, and most patrons feel surprised by this option. Here is where the counselor's skills, creativity, clinical flexibility, and capacity to adapt and to use the setting are crucial to be able to turn the initial sexualized interaction into a possibility for a therapeutic session.

Program formulation

When I was presented with the task of developing a bathhouse counseling program, the challenge was to create an intervention suitable for the particulars of the setting, the intricacies of the population, and with reasonable objectives to meet the requirements of our funders to decrease the transmission of HIV. Funders wanted to reach a population deemed to be "difficult to reach" and to create a step toward accessing appropriate mental health services. We believed that we could do so by creating a space for bathhouse patrons to talk more in-depth about some of the complexities that surround sexual health promotion and cause difficulties in their decision-making process (AIDS Committee of Toronto, 2011; Stall, Friedman, & Catania, 2008).

Psychoanalytic theory seemed like a perfect match to support this kind of intervention, particularly around understanding sexualized environments; unconscious conflict and its role in anxiety and acting out; and understanding and fostering a solid working alliance in a single-session model. I refer to psychoanalysis as both the body of theory as a whole, and a plural set of techniques that aim to expand the persons' knowledge of themselves. At a technical and clinical level, it can help us to develop more tools necessary to foster change and reach marginalized populations (Berzoff et al., 2016; Bolognini, 2011; Freud, 1910, 1913; Tucket, 2008).

We needed to consider that these spaces can trigger intense reactions in the patrons (as well as the counselors) regardless of their sexual orientation and/or sexual identity. Some of these intense forms of anxiety foster defensive maneuvers, such as regression (Freud, 1926; Lapanche & Pontalis, 1973), to cope with some particular forms of traumatic anxiety (Fernando, 2009). For example, the thought of the act of one man having sex with another man can provoke overwhelming anxiety for some of these patrons, due to internalized homophobia, religious beliefs, cultural background, relationship status, etc.

We were thus providing an opportunity to tap into the patron's traumatic anxieties to try to slow down acting out (Fernando, 2009). This was to counterbalance distortions in the patron's judgment due to deficits in ego functioning (Bellak & Meyers, 1975; Berzoff et al., 2016; Bolognini, 2011) or environmental triggers that exacerbated regression (Laplanche & Pontalis, 1973). It would also support the development of a therapeutic alliance that can bridge bathhouse patrons to appropriate community services as needed.

Contrary to common assumptions, a lot of men seem to feel safe in the anonymity of a bathhouse; safe from scrutiny and external judgment. Psychoanalytic theory can help us to understand and benefit from the sense of safety and privacy in the anonymity provided by the bathhouse. We used this sense of safety to support a holding environment that will be crucial for the counseling session. Thinking of the bathhouse as a holding environment that will support a counseling session requires the psychoanalytic clinician to engage with the bathhouse patron in a conversation that will be meaningful for the patron. Through Winnicott's transitional phenomena, the bathhouse can serve as a transitional object, or as a "first possession" (Winnicott, 1953, p. 89) that will enable and drive therapeutic support during the bathhouse counseling session. Within this psychic space in the mind of the patron, the bathhouse provides a holding environment, where psychic maneuvers to manage inner and external realities unfold, and can be put to test.

As we continue to weave Winnicott's ideas of holding environment and transitional phenomena (1945, 1953, 1956 and 1986), the bathhouse counselor's presence operates in the bathhouse setting as a container for the otherwise highly sexualized experience. The fact that there is a counselor with its symbolic representations (service contract agreements, clinical supervision, partnerships) in this setting provides a psychic representation that contains the surplus of overwhelming anxiety in some bathhouse patrons. It normalizes the space, breaks the secret, and makes the space thinkable for the overwhelmed bathhouse patron. The openings for a counseling session become the anchor points for the development of a positive working alliance that can support a psychic space that allows transitional phenomena in a bathhouse session.

The session

Once the session is on its course, the sexualized tone stays present usually throughout the first half of the session. While this can be very anxiety provoking for the counselor, it is the sine qua non of bathhouse interactions. I believe that the sexualized initial interaction and the counselor's response to it, in addition to the fact that patrons remain anonymous all through the session, can provide transference-like qualities that accelerate the establishment of a therapeutic alliance and facilitate disclosure of important material during a session (Greenson & Wexler, 1969; Joseph, 1985). If a need is identified, there is the possibility of follow-up counseling for up to eight sessions at ACT, where the counselor can continue to work with some of the issues identified, and/or streamline referrals for services with some of our community partners (AIDS Committee of Toronto, 2011). I will illustrate this by providing a brief narrative of a common initial sexualized interaction that led to an opening for a session in which the bathhouse patron spoke about feeling guilty for surviving his partner whom he lost to a very aggressive form of cancer:

Bathhouse Patron (BP): Why are you not naked?

Counselor (C): I'm here to talk.

BP: I'm not here to talk; I want to fuck you.

C: Thanks. We can't though. But we can talk? [The counselor explains the scope of the program.]

BP: But what do we talk about? Give me an example.

C: Anything you like. Some guys talk about feeling sad, or guilty, for coming here.

BP: I never feel guilty when I come here.

C: Good. Some guys feel very guilty right after they come, and feel the need to rush out of here.

BP: Oh, that happens to me. Is that guilt?

C: I don't know. Do you want to talk about it?

BP: I guess so. I'm already here, and you are not going to get naked. Is this free?

As you can tell from the opening and the beginning stages of the negotiation of the session, this type of brief intervention is definitely not psychoanalysis proper. Nevertheless, my training and background influence the service provision and how we think about the program. To be able to differentiate significant contacts from actual counseling sessions for research purposes, we called any interaction that happened between a patron and a counselor and lasted less than 10 minutes a "contact," regardless of whether the counselor used his counseling skills. Thus any interaction that lasted between 10 and 45 minutes is considered a "session." During one shift, a counselor can have anywhere from zero to four sessions, lasting between 10 and 45 minutes.

The first year of TowelTalk was from April 12, 2009, to April 11, 2010. During that year we had one counselor in place, and he provided 88 counseling sessions, with an average of 1.2 sessions per shift, the average session lasting 28.2 minutes (AIDS Committee of Toronto, 2011). During this year most of the sessions were single sessions, and although approximately 40% of patrons who accessed Towel Talk were referred to follow-up counseling at ACT, roughly only 10% of those referrals actually followed through. The goal of the sessions is to develop the therapeutic alliance between counselor and patron, to build trust, and to foster a good enough and containing environment for the patron to think about complex issues (Winnicott, 1945, 1958, 1969). As it is consistent with research findings in countertransference (Hayes, 2004) and "common factors" literature (Drisko, 2004; Ravitz &

Maunder, 2015), developing a therapeutic alliance allows the counselor to connect the patron to appropriate services, such as mental health services. A solid therapeutic alliance enables patrons to talk about issues they may not have talked about before (AIDS Committee of Toronto, 2011; Greenson & Wexler, 1969).

Holding environment and transitional phenomena as possibilities in the bathhouse

There are a series of factors that create a hyperstimulating environment in the bathhouse: nudity, anonymity, porn, sexualized atmosphere, music, low lighting, sexual sounds, and body odor. This hyperstimulation can both arouse and threaten the patron, overwhelming him. It is my belief that these factors create a fertile ground for primary-process irruption, unconscious and preconscious id impulses, and their counterparts—early and rigid defenses—to be readily available for bathhouse patrons. These overwhelming experiences do not happen to every single patron who accesses a bathhouse, but it definitely may be part of the experience of many of the patrons that we spoke with during our sessions. Some of these overwhelming experiences may be interpreted by bathhouse patrons in different ways.

The section of the patrons who accessed the program reported becoming overwhelmed due to a conflict being reactivated by the bathhouse setting. For example, one of the most common topics that was reported by bathhouse counselors during their sessions was guilt and shame in connection with the bathhouse (AIDS Committee of Toronto, 2011). These unspoken tensions invest the bathhouse with unique regressive qualities, allowing a patron, who might feel embarrassed and ashamed of having to access the bathhouse, to be capable of overriding feelings of disgust, remorse, and overwhelming guilt by splitting it off and projecting it onto the environment (Carveth, 2010; Fernando, 2009; Freud, 1919; Rosthsteing, 1994). Nevertheless, and agreeing with Rapaport (1953), regression processes bring to the forefront formidable intensity in the effects experienced.

It seems evident to me that regression should be present in such an active environment like a bathhouse, where "acting out" through a series of random, intense, and sometimes compulsive-like connections occurs. This adds to the bathhouse atmosphere a tinge of repetition that can help the counselor in gaining some insight into patrons' inner worlds and unconscious fantasies. I believe this regression experienced as split off, when contained and provided meaning, can be a very useful tool to foster a transitional space that makes the bathhouse room a space conducive for psychotherapeutic counseling. A psychoanalytic-informed intervention in a bathhouse setting can help provide a possibility for symbolization of very anxiety-provoking experiences for men. When the patron is overwhelmed by unconscious affects, repetition compulsion, and primary-process irruption, the counselor can help him to slow down by introducing secondary processes and a space to think and reflect.

Paradoxically, it is this regressive quality of the environment that I think supports my hypothesis that psychoanalytically informed interventions within a single- session model in a bathhouse can be effective attempts to achieve the goals of the session and the program objectives. It is my belief that regression lies behind the session's openings. Once a counselor has identified an opening and helps the patron feel comfortable enough to explore an issue with him, disclosures of emotionally charged material frequently take place. These emotional disclosures usually follow the initial sexualized interaction that I mentioned before. Suddenly, the initial sexualized interaction unveils the patron's attempts to manage anxiety by sexualizing it; and his struggle to get close to the counselor, while at the same time trying to push him away.

The appropriate management of the sexualized initial stage of the session by the counselor can help him fast-track the construction of a solid-like therapeutic alliance that aids in the process of making referrals for community services and/or follow-up counseling. For example, the moment a patron discloses that he or she experiences the analyst as a possible sexual object is very dramatic. It usually threatens the continuation of the analysis, and it evokes a "make it or break it" moment. In the bathhouse, this statement happens from the get-go. In my experience, once a patron attempts to cross that boundary without feeling hostile rejection and shame from the counselor it sets a precedent in the mind of the patron. This action operates as an interpretation that contains the aggressive qualities of the sexual proposition and holds the space for symbolization. The bathhouse resonates louder as a holding environment for the bathhouse patron seeking a connection.

Boundaries are kindly but firmly restated, modeling what a therapeutic interaction inside of a bathhouse would look like for the patron: walking inside and outside of the transitional space, negotiating the boundaries, and practicing the forms of early communication. The patron is faced by a calm and understanding counselor who is receptive. This lays the groundwork for trust, as the counselor conveys a warm tolerance that reaffirms his presence as a possible benign object, who is not easy to scandalize, manipulate, or destroy (Winnicott, 1969). I believe this is another precursor of the intense emotional disclosures that can unfold during a TowelTalk session. These disclosures usually relate to trauma, abuse (childhood, emotional, psychological, or physical abuse), severe experiences of emotional deprivation, loneliness and isolation, relationship difficulties, etc. (e.g., bathhouse counseling session theme on AIDS Committee of Toronto [2011]). This sparks curiosity in the patron, and allows him to make use of the counselor (Winnicott, 1969). This brings up the feeling in the counselor that the therapeutic process and emotional disclosures can happen very quickly in a bathhouse session, in contrast to my clinical experience providing brief and long-term psychotherapy and conducting analysis. I believe this sensation is how the counselor experiences the patron's anxiety and the bathhouse regressive qualities (the sexualized atmosphere) in the countertransference. It is the counselor's reactions to the bathhouse regression and the patron's disavowed anxiety, and how he uses it for the benefit of the patron, that can impact the session. This impact creates a moment where both patron and counselor slow down enough to think about distressing thoughts and affects. Both of them are holding the space, keeping the boundaries in place and moving forward the therapeutic action.

Trauma in the bathhouse

Here I elaborate further on some hypotheses as to why we were able to have such meaningful disclosures within a single-session model. I believe we were able to connect so fast because of the bathhouse setting. Here it is important to draw on ideas from trauma treatment from a psychoanalytic and integrative perspective (Davies & Frawley, 1994; Herman, 1992; Rothschild, 2000). In a nutshell, the central nervous system gets overwhelmed and shuts down parts of the brain to prevent damage from stress hormones. The bathhouse patron may in fact not have the words to explain his experience or his needs, or to negotiate sexual boundaries due to the overwhelming anxiety that shuts down parts of his thinking process, priming him to act out in order to regulate the internal experience (Rothschild, 2000). In addition to the environmental factors and the patrons' proneness to anxiety, I would like to add Fernando's concept of the "zero process" (2012). According to him, thoughts that trigger traumatic anxiety can be overwhelming to the point of shutting down thought processes. This shutting down impacts not only the anxiety-provoking thought, but any association connected to it. These thoughts and associations are split off and rendered inaccessible for the client.

For example, some men reported difficulties with their own definition of sexual orientation and sexual identity (AIDS Committee of Toronto, 2011). Some men, while in the bathhouse, are not able to think or elaborate on any material that might touch on the idea of two men having sex, and any association to it. The mere thought elicits an unbearable amount of anxiety and guilt. Different factors might be involved; they could be married to women or be in closed, monogamous, and committed relationships with men. As well, their cultural and/or religious background may contribute to this intrapsychic conflict. Either way, they are unable to process, integrate, symbolize, or abstract important information available in the bathhouse. This has a direct impact on their judgment, as they are not able to think and anticipate risks before acting out, rendering the more typical HIV prevention campaigns useless.

When the bathhouse counselor meets with a bathhouse patron as the patron is overwhelmed by the experience of the bathhouse, the counselor can help the patron to symbolize part of the overwhelming aspects of the bathhouse, containing it and detoxifying it. The counselor operates in the bathhouse setting as an environmental mother who allows use of the bathhouse setting in a therapeutic way (Winnicott, 1945, 1953). The following provides a clinical example of this.

Clinical excerpt

Mr. X, a 65-year-old white man, approached the bathhouse counselor and complimented him on his resemblance to a famous male TV actor from the 1980s. The counselor thought it was a cheesy pickup line. He noticed feeling disgusted with the patron's contrastingly less sexualized remark than the customary "I want to fuck you" that some patrons say. He then felt an urgent need to want to "get rid of the patron." In "Primitive Emotional Development" (1945), Winnicott speaks about the caregiver's capacity to hold the unrepresented bits and pieces of the incohesive baby. This allowed the counselor some room to stay with the disgust and not identify with it, effectively containing the counselor's need to get rid of Mr. X. The counselor proceeded as usual and described the scope of the program in a tone that clearly overcompensated the counselor's feelings of guilt with kindness toward the patron. We believed this was an unconscious attempt by the counselor to repair the guilt experienced by the conscious thought of wanting to get rid of a prospective client.

Mr. X declined the invitation to speak, but kept walking around the area where the counselor was standing, giving the impression of cruising the counselor, occasionally winking and smiling at the counselor every time he walked past him. Although the counselor reported in supervision that he felt "annoyed at the childish attempts to desperately seek his attention," he noticed feeling uncomfortably aroused. It was this contrasting experience of intense feelings that led the counselor to stop the bathhouse patron and ask him whether he wanted to speak and if he would like to tell him more about the TV actor of the 1980s. Mr. X did not decline the invitation this time, and a conversation about Magnum PI paved the way for a session about Mr. X's mother's death anniversary on exactly that day one year ago. According to Mr. X, he was carrying his mother's full bottle of prescription sleeping pills, and was planning to take all of them with a bottle of vodka and pass out in the whirlpool. He said, "You would be surprised of the times that I have been unnoticed in this place." Mr. X went to his room and brought the bottle of pills and the bottle of vodka and handed them to the counselor. "What made you change your mind?" the counselor asked. Mr. X replied, "You were not disgusted by me. You were very kind and patient, and you smiled."

Conclusion and recommendations for clinical social work practice

Psychoanalytic theory has opened the door for us to explore how we can think about complex human experiences such as human sexuality, diversity, relationships, and conflicts. It can bring insight into the realm of clinical social work and community-based practice. This insight can help us understand diverse communities with complex needs that have fallen through the cracks of our mental health care system, and how to adapt psychoanalytic theory to inform community-based interventions. This, to me, is the simplest form of psychoanalytic outreach, to make psychoanalytically informed interventions accessible to community members.

TowelTalk is a collaborative intervention geared to reach gay, bisexual, and other MSM in their community. It brings a mental health intervention to the community, to a setting that outwardly seems not to be conducive for counseling. Although TowelTalk currently has not settled on a specific model for its intervention, I explored some of the benefits of using a psychoanalytic approach while trying to implement a therapeutic counseling program in a bathhouse. Psychoanalysis is the only body of knowledge that deals with sexualized trauma and sexualized defenses patients employ to deal with trauma in depth. It provides a wealth of concepts that allow for flexibility and adaptability in the bathhouse counselor and facilitates understanding of complex internal experiences of the bathhouse patrons.

Further work is needed to answer important questions like the effectiveness of a single-session intervention in a bathhouse; clinical implications of the transference and countertransference dynamics in the bathhouse; the impact of this type of work, and the possible counter-phobic defensive reactions arising in the counselors to cope with the intensity of the bathhouse; clinical implications for boundaries;

etc. Finally, it is important to also understand how to bridge these findings back to an analytic proper setting.

Acknowledgment

I greatly appreciate the invaluable support of the AIDS Committee of Toronto, and TowelTalk's funder the AIDS Bureau.

References

Akhtar, S. (1995). A third individuation: Immigration, identity, and the psychoanalytic process. *Journal of the American Psychoanalytic Association*, 43, 1051–1084. doi:10.1177/000306519504300406

Akhtar, S. (2014). The mental pain of minorities. *British Journal of Psychotherapy,* 30, 136–153. doi:10.1111/bjp.12081

Altmann, M., Fitzpatrick-Hanly, M. A., & Leuzinger-Bohleber, M. (2012). Project committee on clinical observation panels12. *International Journal of Psycho-Analysis,* 93, 748–750. doi:10.1111/j.1745-8315.2012.00570.x

Aron, Lews & Starr, K. (2013). *A psychotherapy for the people: Toward a progressive psycho-analysis.* NY: Routledge.

Baranger, M., & Baranger, W. (2008). The analytic situation as a dynamic field. *International Journal of Psycho-Analysis*, 89(4), 795–826. doi:10.1111/j.1745-8315.2008.00074.x

Bellak, L., & Meyers, B. (1975). Ego function assessment and analysability. *International Review of Psycho-Analysis*, 2, 413–427.

Bernardi, R. (1992). On pluralism in psychoanalysis. *Psychoanalytic Inquiry*, 12(4), 506–525. doi:10.1080/07351699209533910

Berzoff, J., Flanagan, L. M., & Hertz, P. (2016). *Inside out and outside in: Psychodynamic clinical theory and psychopathology in contemporary multicultural contexts* (4 ed.). New Jersey: Jason Aronson/Roman Littlefield.

Bingham, C. (2002). On Paulo Freire's debt to psychoanalysis: Authority on the side of freedom. *Studies in Philosophy and Education,* 21(6), 447–464. doi:10.1023/A:1020861224138

Bleger, J. (1974). Schizophrenia, autism, and symbiosis. *Contemporary Psychoanalysis,* 10, 19– 25. doi:10.1080/00107530.1974.10745308

Bleger, J. (2013). El concepto de psicosis. Area 3 Cuadernos de TemasGrupales e Institucionales. No. 17. Retrieved from http://www.area3.org.es/Uploads/a3-17-conceptopsicosis.JBleger.pdf

Bolognini, S. (2011). La función social del psicoanálisis. *RevistaPsicoanánlisis de la Asociación Psicoanalítica de Madrid*, 62, 221–226.

Busch, F. N., Milrod, B. L., & Sandberg, L.S. (2009). A study demonstrating efficacy of a psychoanalytic psychotherapy for panic disorder: Implications for psychoanalytic research, theory, & practice. *Journal of the American Psychoanalysis Association.*, 57, 131–148. doi:10.1177/ 0003065108329677

Carveth, D.L. (2010). Superego, conscience, and the nature and types of guilt. *Modern Psychoanalysis; New York,* Vol. 35, Iss. 1, 106-130,144.

Cassorla, R.M. (2005). From bastion to enactment. *International Journal of Psycho-Analysis*, 86 (3), 699–719. doi:10.1516/RR33-A8FH-V4RB-CDXJ

Cattaneo, J., Cain, R., Cullen, J., Dolan, L., Hart, T., Le, D. ... Posadas, M. (2009). Examining new interventions in unconventional settings: Counselling in Toronto's male bathhouses. *Canadian Journal of Infectious Diseases and Medical Microbiology*, 21(Suppl B), 30B (Abstract).

Cattaneo, J., Cain, R., Cullen, J., Hart, T. A. & Murray, J: AIDS Committee of Toronto. (2011). *TowelTalk Evaluation Report 2009–2010*. Toronto, ON

Davids, M. F. (2003). The internal racist. *Bulletin of the British Psychoanalytical Society*, 39(4), 1–15.

Davies, J. M., & Frawley, M. G. (1994). Treating the adult survivor of childhood sexual abuse: *A Psychoanalytic Perspective*. New York: Basic Books.

Drisko, J. (2004). "Common factors" in psychotherapy outcome: Meta-analytic findings and their implications for practice and research. *Families in Society,* 85(1), 81–90. doi:10.1606/ 1044-3894.239

Esman, A. (Eds). (1990). *Essential papers on transference*. New York: New York University Press.

Fernando, J. (2009). *The processes of defense: Trauma, drives, and reality – a new synthesis*. Toronto: Jason Aronson.

Fernando, J. (2012). Trauma and the zero process. *Canadian Journal of Psychoanalysis*, 20(2), 267–290.

Freire, P. (1970). *Pedagogy of the oppressed*. London: Bloomsbury.

Freud, S. (1905). Three essays on the theory of sexuality. *The Standard Edition of the Complete Psychological Works of Sigmund Freud, Volume VII (1901-1905): A Case of Hysteria, Three Essays on Sexuality and Other Works.* 123–246.

Freud, S. (1908). On the sexual theories of children. *The standard edition of the complete psychological works of Sigmund Freud, volume IX (1906-1908): Jensen's 'Gradiva' and other works.* 205–226.

Freud, S. (1910). The future prospects of psycho-analytic therapy. *The standard edition of the complete psychological works of Sigmund Freud, volume XI (1910): Five lectures on psycho- analysis, Leonardo da Vinci and other works.* 139–152.

Freud, S. (1912). The dynamics of transference. *The standard edition of the complete psychological works of Sigmund Freud, volume XII (1911–1913): The case of Schreber, papers on technique and other works.*

Freud, S. (1913). On beginning the treatment (Further recommendations on the technique of psycho-analysis I). *The standard edition of the complete psychological works of Sigmund Freud, volume XII (1911–1913): The case of Schreber, papers on technique and other works.* 121–144.

Freud, S. (1915). Observations on transference-love (Further recommendations on the technique of psycho-analysis III). *The standard edition of the complete psychological works of Sigmund Freud, volume XII (1911–1913): The Case of Schreber, papers on technique and other works.* 157–171.

Freud, S. (1919). Lines of advance in psycho-analytic therapy. *The standard edition of the complete psychological works of Sigmund Freud, volume XVII (1917–1919): An infantile neurosis and other works.* 157–168.

Freud, S. (1925). Some psychical consequences of the anatomical distinction between the sexes. *The standard edition of the complete psychological works of Sigmund Freud, volume XIX (1923–1925): The ego and the id and other works.* 241–258.

Freud, S. (1926). Inhibitions, symptoms and anxiety. *The standard edition of the complete psychological works of Sigmund Freud (Vol 20, pp. 75–176).*

Freud, S. (1931). Female sexuality. *The standard edition of the complete psychological works of Sigmund Freud, volume XXI (1927–1931): The future of an illusion, civilization and its discontents, and other works.* 221–244.

Freud, S. (1933). New introductory lectures on psycho-analysis. *The standard edition of the complete psychological works of Sigmund Freud, volume XXII (1932–1936): New introductory lectures on psycho-analysis and other works.* 1–182.

Gallo, R. (2010). *Freud's Mexico: Into the wilds of psychoanalysis.* The MIT Press.

Glocer Fiorini, L. (2017). *Sexual difference in debate: Bodies, desires, and fictions.* London: Karnac.

Goldstein, E. (2009). The Relationship between social work and psychoanalysis: The future impact of social workers. *Clinical Social Work Journal,* 37, 7–13. doi:10.1007/s10615–007-0090–8

Greenson, R. R., & Wexler, M. (1969). The non-transference relationship in the psycho-analytic situation. *International Journal of Psycho-Analysis,* 50, 27–39.

Hayes, J. A. (2004). The inner world of the psychotherapist: A program of research on countertransference. *Psychotherapy Research,* 14(1), 21–36. doi:10.1093/ptr/kph002

Herman, J. L. (1992). *Trauma and Recovery.* New York: Harper Collins: Basic Books.

Herzog, D. (2015). What happened to psychoanalysis in the wake of the sexual revolution? A story about the durability of homophobia and the dream of love, 19500s- 2010. In A., Lemma &

Lynch, P. (Eds.) (2015), *Sexualities: Contemporary Psychoanalytic Perspectives.* London: Routledge.

Joseph, B. (1985). Transference: The total situation. *International Journal of Psycho-Analysis,* 66, 447–454. Kantor, J. (In Press). El Superyó Piel: Psicoanálisis y Racismo. Peru.

Laplanche, J., & Pontalis, J.-B. (1973). *The Language of Psycho-Analysis.* New York: W. W. Norton & Company, Inc.

Leary, K. (2007). Racial insult and repair. *Psychoanalytic Dialogues,* 17(4), 539–549. doi:10.1080/ 10481880701487292

Lemma, A., Target, M., & Fonagy, P. (2010). The development of a brief psychodynamic protocol for depression: Dynamic Interpersonal Therapy (DIT). *Psychoanalytic Psychotherapy,* 24, 329–346. doi:10.1080/02668734.2010.513547

Leuzinger-Bohleber, M. (2004). What does conceptual research have to offer?. *International Journal of Psycho-Analysis,* 85, 1477–1478. doi:10.1516/TABK-E55U-D6J6-YWCY

Leuzinger-Bohleber, M., Stuhrast, U., Ruger, B., & Beutel, M. (2003). How to study the 'quality of psychoanalytic treatments' and their long-term effects on patients' well- being. *International Journal of Psycho-Analysis,* 84, 263–290. doi:10.1516/C387–0AFM-4P34-M4BT

Loewenberg, P., & Thompson, N. L. (Eds). (2011). 100 Year of the IPA: *The Centenary History of the International Psychoanalytical Association 1910 – 2010 Evolution and Change.* London: Karnac. Malberg, N. T.,

Fonagy, P., & Mayes, L. (2008). Contemporary psychoanalysis in a pediatric hemodialysis unit development of a mentalization-based group intervention for adolescent patients with end-stage renal disease. *Annual Psychoanalysis,* 36, 101–114.

Moss, D. (2001). On hating in the first person plural. *Journal of the American Psychoanalytic Association,* 49, 1315–1334. doi:10.1177/00030651010490041801

Mullaly, B. (2002). *Challenging oppression: A critical social work approach.* New York, Oxford University Press.

Leuzinger-Bohleber, M., & Pfenning, N. (2010). The Medea Fantasy: An inevitable burden during prenatal diagnostics? *The International Journal of Psychoanalysis,* 91(5), 1227–1230. https://doi.org/10.1111/j.1745-8315.2010.00330.x

Perlman, F. T. (1994). The professional identity of the social work-psychoanalyst: The genesis of professional identity. *Psychoanalytic Social Work,* 2(1), 67–98. doi:10.1300/ j408v02n01_05

Ramirez, S. (1978). *El Mexicano, psicología de sus motivaciones.* Mexico: Editorial Grijalbo.

Rapaport, D. (1953). On the psycho-analytic theory of affects. *International Journal of Psycho- Analysis,* 24, 177–198.

Rasmussen, B., & Salhani, D. (2010). A contemporary kleinian contribution to understanding racism. *Social Service Review,* 84(3), 491–513. doi:10.1086/656401

Ravitz, P., & Maunder, R. (Eds). (2015). *Achieving Psychotherapy Effectiveness.* New York: W. W. Norton & Company, Inc.

Rothstein, A. M. (1994). Shame and the Superego. *Psychoanalytic Study of the Child,* 49, 263– 277.

Rothschild, Babette. (2000). *The Body Remembers: The psychophysiology of trauma and trauma treatment.* New York, NY: WWNorton.

Roughton, R. E. (2002). Rethinking homosexuality. *Journal of the American Psychoanalytic Association*, 50, 733–763. doi:10.1177/00030651020500032001 Sakamoto, I., &

Pitner, R. (2005). Use of critical consciousness in anti-oppressive social work practice: Disentangling power dynamics at personal and structural levels. *British Journal of Social Work*, 35, 435–452. doi:10.1093/bjsw/bch190

Soler, C. (2007). *Estudios Sobre las Psicosis.* Buenos Aires: Manantial.

Stall, R., Friedman, M., & Catania, J.A. (2008). Interacting epidemics and gay men's health: A theory of syndemic production among urban gay men. In R.J., Wolitski, R., Stall, & R. O., Valdiserri (Eds.), *Unequal opportunities: Health disparities affecting gay and bisexual men in the United States* (pp. 251–273). New York: Oxford University Press.

Stone, L. (1954). The widening scope of indications for psychoanalysis. *Journal of the American Psychoanalytical Association, 2*, 567–594.

Suchet, M. (2007). Unraveling whiteness. *Psychoanalytic Dialogues, 17*, 867–886. doi:10.1080/10481880701703730

Swenson, C. (1994). Freud's "Anna O.": Social work's Bertha Pappenheim. *Clinical Social Work, 22*(2), 149–163. doi:10.1007/BF02190471

Tuckett, D. (2008). *Psychoanalysis comparable and incomparable: The evolution of a method to describe and compare psychoanalytic approaches.* London: Routledge.

Williams, C. (2002). A rationale for an anti-racist entry point to anti-oppressive social work in mental health services. *Critical Social Work, 2*:(2), 20–31.

Winnicott, D. W. (1945). Primitive emotional development. *International Journal of Psycho- Analysis, 26*, 137–143.

Winnicott, D.W. (1949). Hate in the counter-transference. *International Journal of Psycho-Analysis, 30*, 69–74.

Winnicott, D. W. (1953). Transitional objects and transitional phenomena—A study of the first not-me possession. *International Journal of Psycho-Analysis, 34*, 89–97.

Winnicott, D. W. (1956). Primary maternal preoccupation. In *Winnicott (1958) Collected Papers* (pp. 300–3005). New York: Basic Books.

Winnicott, D. W. (1958). *Collected Papers.* New York: Basic Books.

Winnicott, D. W. (1969). The use of an object. *International Journal of Psycho-Analysis, 50*, 711–716.

Winnicott, D. W. (1986). Holding and Interpretation. *Holding and Interpretation: Fragment of An Analysis.* 115, 1–194. London: The Hogarth Press and the Institute of Psycho-Analysis.

Wolstein, B. (Eds). (1988). *Essential papers on countertransference.* New York: New York University Press.

Wolstein, B. (1997). The first direct analysis of transference and countertransference. *Psychoanalytic Inquiry, 17*, 505–521. doi:10.1080/07351699709534145

Can You Be Trauma-Informed If You're Not Thinking About the Unconscious Processes in Your Practice?

RAHIM THAWER, MSW, RSW

As the summer of 2010 approached, I was preparing to fly from Canada to Australia for the months of June, July and August. Despite it being winter in the southern hemisphere, I was eager to take hold of a unique international MSW practicum opportunity at an organization in Melbourne. My task for the placement was to conduct a literature review on exploring what it means to be trauma-informed at all levels of an organization. Additionally, I co-developed an organization-wide survey and then conducted interviews with case managers and psychotherapists. The service user programs targeted people with serious mental illness and co-occurring substance use disorders, sex workers, and people who were economically marginalized. The practicum culminated in a final report and presentation I gave at a town hall of all employees across the four sites of the host organization.

I drew on some critical literature to help me do this work. The main resource I consulted was from the journal *New Directions for Mental Health Services*, co-edited by Maxine Harris and Roger Fallot, and entitled *Using trauma theory to design service systems (2001)*. The following table of contents of this 89th volume eventually became a cornerstone of my social work education and set the groundwork for future practice:

1. Envisioning a trauma-informed service system: a vital paradigm shift

2. A trauma-informed approach to screening and assessment

3. Trauma-informed inpatient services

4. Trauma-informed approaches to housing

5. Designing trauma-informed addictions services

6. Trauma-informed services and case management

7. Defining the role of consumer-survivors in trauma-informed systems

8. Care of the clinician

Additionally, a paper entitled *Trauma-informed or trauma-denied: Principles and implementation of trauma-informed services for women* (Elliot et al., 2005), helped me to synthesize my organizational survey data into clear recommendations for practice.

Using trauma theory to design service systems: a summary

In the realm of social work and psychotherapy, the evolution towards trauma-informed care represents a paradigm shift, or a reorientation, from asking, "What's wrong with you?" to "What happened to you?" At the core of trauma-informed care is the recognition that the vast majority of clients seeking help have a history of trauma, and this history plays a crucial role in their current functioning and interaction with service systems.

Being trauma-informed means recognizing that individuals often develop coping mechanisms, such as substance abuse or other problematic behaviors, as adaptations to trauma (or what Gestalt therapists call 'creative adjustments'). This view helps to shift the stance of the caregiver from one of judgment to one of empathy and understanding. It re-frames maladaptive behaviors not as the problem itself but as survival strategies that emerged in response to traumatic experiences.

Trauma-informed social work is a client-centered approach that emphasizes trust, safety, respect, collaboration, hope and shared power. It moves beyond the symptom-focused model and integrates knowledge about trauma into service delivery, ensuring that interactions and treatments do not inadvertently re-traumatize the client.

The development of trauma-informed thinking acknowledges the complex relationship between trauma and issues like addiction. It calls for a holistic understanding of the individual, considering the neurological, biological, psychological, and social aspects of their lives. This integrative approach is vital, especially in fields like addiction services, where treatments often need to be gender-specific (or population-focused) and responsive to the unique needs of individuals, such as women who have historically been underserved by programs designed primarily for male service users.

A trauma-informed approach requires a shift in programmatic structure to ensure that the professional addresses the needs of the whole person. It seeks to address symptoms of trauma and the consequences of addiction within a single model of care, fostering an environment that promotes empowerment, relationship building and healing for the service user.

There are five key principles that guide trauma-informed practice:

1. Safety: Creating both physical and emotional safety for clients. A safe environment allows for trust to develop and for personal information to be disclosed at a comfortable pace for the client.

2. Trustworthiness: Establishing clear expectations and consistency is crucial. This means being transparent in practices and policies and maintaining a boundary between the survivor and the therapist that is both firm and flexible, responsive to the unique needs of each client.

3. Choice: Empowering clients by giving them control over their recovery process is essential. It involves respecting their right to make decisions about their care and participation in treatment.

4. Collaboration: Working with clients as partners in the healing process. This involves validating clients' experiences, working together to develop coping strategies and building a support network.

5. Empowerment: Fostering empowerment throughout the program or service. This means emphasizing the client's strengths, providing opportunities for skill development, and reinforcing the belief that recovery is possible.

The trauma-informed approach also involves educating clients about the intersection of trauma and substance use, helping them understand the role of triggers and the function of symptoms (e.g. substance use, impulsivity, dissociation, withdrawal, etc.) as self-soothing strategies. By contextualizing behaviors and relationship patterns within the client's life experiences and trauma history, the social worker or psychotherapist is laying a foundation for recovery without risking the retraumatization of the client, even if it is unconscious (Freud, 1923).

Therefore, a trauma-informed social worker or psychotherapist must hold a deep understanding of the pervasive impact of trauma and the complex ways in which it interweaves with various life domains.

This includes unconscious processes in the clinician and unconscious dynamics between the social worker and client that may impact the positive outcomes of the treatment. The ultimate goal is to provide a service delivery that is sensitive, empathetic and empowering, thereby aiding clients in their journey toward healing and recovery.

What is the unconscious?

The concept of the unconscious, as initially laid out by Sigmund Freud (1923), describes it as a repository for thoughts, desires, and memories that are inaccessible to the conscious mind due to their unsettling nature, leading to repression. Anna Freud (1936) elaborated on the dynamics of the unconscious, particularly focusing on defense mechanisms employed by the ego (the conscious mediator, helps make decisions) to manage conflicts between the id (pleasure-seeking, can be impulsive) and the superego (moral compass, can be judgemental). Melanie Klein (1946) further contributed by emphasizing the role of early object relationships in the formation of the unconscious, with fantasies and internalized images of self and others developed in infancy shaping one's psychic landscape. Carl Jung (1968) expanded the concept by introducing the collective unconscious, comprising universal archetypes shared among individuals, suggesting the unconscious is not only personal but also collective.

Together, these theorists provide a foundation for understanding the unconscious as a complex and dynamic interplay of personal and collective elements shaped by early relational experiences and the ongoing negotiation of psychological conflicts.

Contemporary psychoanalyst Nancy McWilliams (2011) adds that the unconscious encompasses repressed material and undeveloped, disavowed, or dissociated aspects of the self. She highlights the relational dimension of the unconscious, suggesting that our relationships and interactions with others significantly influence it. McWilliams suggests that the unconscious develops through a blend of innate predispositions and the internalization of relational experiences.

When we unconsciously re-traumatized a client: a vignette

Fast forward to fall 2017 in Toronto. The walls of an inner city health center echoed with quiet stories of healing and pain. It was here, amidst the gentle hustle of a family health team, that a narrative unfolded, one that lingers in my memory for its poignant simplicity.

As a staff therapist and clinical supervisor, I found myself guiding another cohort of healers. Among them was a therapist trainee — a mature student whose life experiences had shaped her into a vessel of empathy, brimming with an eagerness to delve into the intricate world of trauma-focused therapy. She stepped into her practicum placement, her eyes alight with the eagerness of a beginner and the wisdom of a seasoned soul.

Assigned to her care was a client whose past had been etched with the scars of neglect. This individual, grown yet still haunted by the shadows of childhood, spoke of days marred by hunger—a cruel punishment for minor infractions. The client had meals withheld from her as punishment and pet food served to her at times to humiliate her. This individual's humanity was often forgotten amidst the turmoil of a home where love was eclipsed by violence. She shared a dream with her therapist, simple yet profound—the longing for a family dinner, for a taste of a true Thanksgiving feast, an experience so ordinary yet so achingly out of reach.

During their sessions, the topic of Thanksgiving arose, and the therapist, perhaps without thinking it through, disclosed her own plans—a gathering and a dish she was to bring as a form of sharing with her client. The client, eyes glimmering with a shard of hope, inquired about the "stuffing," that quintessential element of the feast she had longed for. Sensing the depth of this longing, the therapist offered to bring her some, a gesture seemingly small yet laden with meaning.

Their therapy sessions continued as usual as the holiday weekend approached: a dance of words and silences, of tears and insight. The Canadian Thanksgiving long weekend arrived. The following Tuesday, the therapist, emerging from a draining weekend, arrived at work with her mind clouded, her thoughts on simply surviving the day. It was only upon seeing her client, a figure of quiet anticipation in the waiting room, that the dreadful realization dawned upon her: she had forgotten the stuffing, another unconscious act on the part of the clinician.

The client, once animated with hope, turned to stone, her disappointment a shadow that filled the room. She cried in session in a way that one would expect at the funeral of a beloved. The session that followed was a pilgrimage through pain, a mirror to the neglect that had withered her past. The therapist, without thinking, had hurt the client. She was filled with guilt as she tried to navigate the tides of an effective apology. In supervision, she stood before me, her oversight laid bare without her being able to recognize the unconscious processes that motivated her disclosure and how that perhaps unnecessary disclosure pushed her to participate in a traumatic repetition for her client. I pondered aloud the subtleties of the unconscious mind, its silent but powerful sway over our actions.

I could have lectured her on the nature of boundary crossings and violations, and on the dangers of accepting and/or exchanging gifts. But that would only activate her defenses (i.e. undoing, rationalization, reaction formation). While self-punishment might reduce guilt, it doesn't teach any new lessons in clinical practice. And so, we stood, trainee and supervisor, at the threshold of understanding what had just taken place, to begin re-tracing where the seeds that pushed her to action were planted, and how that led to re-traumatization.

In the trainee, I saw the echo of my own educational journey—a path well trod but lacking in clear curricular materials that explored the role of the unconscious, that mysterious player in the theatre of the mind. The concepts of transference (unconscious relational patterns transferred into the social worker) and countertransference (any thought, idea, feeling, or experience in the mind or body of the clinician that happens during the session and through the work with each client) were being introduced in the placement setting. However, it was much too late to now begin teaching—instead of merely exploring in supervision—the psychoanalytic concepts of projective identification (an unconscious defense mechanism in the adult that stems from earlier childhood experiences of non-verbal communication between the baby and the caregivers), enactments (conscious, pre-conscious or unconscious traumatic repetitions) and unconscious role responsiveness. That's when the question dawned on me: can we really be trauma-informed if we're not thinking about the role of the unconscious for each therapeutic dyad?

Theories of unconscious process and enactments

In this section, I describe two theories about unconscious processes and explore the concept of enactments. This is specifically the curricular material that needs to be taught in any program that seeks to be trauma-informed.

First, the psychoanalytic concept called 'repetition compulsion,' which was first introduced by Freud in 1914 and became the focus of "Beyond the Pleasure Principle" in 1920 (Laplanche and Pontalis, 1973). It refers to a psychological phenomenon in which an individual repeats a traumatic event or its circumstances over and over again. This includes re-enacting or unconsciously/pre-consciously repeating the trauma through their behavior without conscious awareness of the fact that they're repeating historical patterns (Cherry, K., 2023).

Freud elaborated on this notion — the compulsion to unconsciously repeat historical experiences that express the person and the clinician's unconscious desires — in his 1920 essay "Beyond the Pleasure Principle." He observed that individuals would often relive painful experiences or engage in behaviors that led back to difficult situations, even when it seemed to go against their own best interests and desire for happiness, which is guided by the pleasure principle—the instinct to seek pleasure and avoid pain (Akhtar & O'Neil, 2011; Laplanche & Pontalis, 1973).

In relation to trauma, repetition compulsion can be seen in the way that individuals may unconsciously set up repetitive situations that mirror their past traumatogenic experience. This may be an attempt to gain mastery over the original traumatic situation. Unfortunately, it often leads to harm instead of healing. Freud's concept of repetition compulsion deals with an individual's internal struggle with both their inner world and their environment (Akhtar & O'Neil, 2011).

Joseph Sandler's theory of unconscious role responsiveness (Sandler & Sandler, 1998) examines the way individuals may unconsciously take on roles or respond to the expectations and projections of others in a way that is consistent with their own internalized object relationships and conflicts. In their reference guide, *Psychotherapy Essentials To Go: Achieving Psychotherapy Effectiveness*, Pain et al. (2015) locate discussions about this type of unconscious exchange under the subsection "Understanding traumatic experiences and promoting acceptance and integration." When we talk about unconscious exchanges between the patient and therapist, the context of trauma is particularly significant.

For example, if a client has unresolved issues with a critical and emotionally distant parent, they might start reacting to the therapist as if the therapist were critical and distant, even if the therapist is actually warm and supportive. The client might become overly defensive or seek excessive approval from the therapist, replaying the dynamics they experienced in their childhood. In another case, a client who has experienced bullying might unconsciously "provoke" the therapist into a position of authority or criticism, mirroring the dynamic with the bully. The therapist, if aware of this dynamic, can help the client explore these feelings and reactions, providing a corrective emotional experience. In each of these examples, in order to attend to the patient's trauma appropriately, the therapist must think about the unconscious role they are playing out.

This theory emphasizes the interactive nature of relationships, where each person's behavior is a response to the other's behavior, often in a manner that is shaped by past experiences. Rather than focusing on the internal struggle of the clinician, it considers the reciprocal nature of interactions. This dynamic is particularly evident in the therapeutic setting, where the psychotherapist may be unaware of an unconscious inclination to respond to the client in a way that is consistent with the client's relational patterns and expectations and the clinician's own unresolved moments within their personal histories.

The result: enactments led by the clinician that put into play intense emotional experiences acted in the transference and countertransference dynamics (Chused, 1991; Gabbard, 1995; Posadas, 2023).

Enactments can occur when the unconscious role responses of both the therapist and the patient interact in the therapeutic relationship, often mirroring past relationship dynamics (Frayn, 1996). Here are some examples of what this can look like:

Enactment of Dependency: Imagine a patient named Sarah who had a distant and neglectful father during her childhood. She may have unconsciously developed a role of seeking validation and care from authority figures. In therapy, Sarah might unintentionally adopt the role of a dependent person, looking to the therapist for validation and support. On the therapist's side, if they had a nurturing tendency, they might unconsciously adopt a role of being overly supportive and protective. This dynamic could create an enactment where the therapist becomes a parental figure, and Sarah becomes dependent on their approval.

Enactment of Defiance: Consider a patient named Max who grew up with strict and controlling parents. Max might have developed an unconscious role of rebelling against authority. In therapy, they might challenge the therapist's suggestions or resist interventions, which mirrors their historical pattern of defiance. The therapist, unconsciously influenced by their role as an authoritative figure, might react defensively or become more directive. This interaction could lead to an enactment where the therapist and patient engage in a power struggle resembling Max's past dynamics.

Enactment of Dismissiveness: John, a patient, had a critical mother during childhood. He might have internalized a role of dismissing emotions and avoiding vulnerability. In therapy, he might downplay his feelings or avoid discussing sensitive topics. The therapist, following their role as a professional, might also downplay emotions and focus on intellectual analysis. This could result in an enactment where emotional exploration is avoided, replicating John's habitual pattern of emotional detachment.

Enactments can be turned into opportunities for providing valuable insights into the patient's unconscious patterns and unresolved conflicts. Therapists can recognize these patterns and use them as opportunities for exploration and intervention (e.g., interpretations, reconstructions, hypotheses, new narratives, etc.). By addressing these enactments, therapists and patients can work together to understand how past experiences influence their roles and behavior, ultimately promoting healing and personal growth.

Re-traumatization in the therapy

In their textbook, *Treating the trauma survivor: An essential guide to trauma-informed care*, Clark et al (2015) dedicate a chapter to exploring the depths of transference and countertransference in the context of trauma treatment. The authors discuss "Karpman's Triangle" in the context of the therapeutic relationship.

The Karpman Triangle, also known as the Drama Triangle, is a social model of human interaction proposed by Stephen Karpman. His original paper (1968) outlines three habitual psychological roles (or stances) that people often take in response to a situation, especially within the context of conflict or "drama." The roles are victim, rescuer and persecutor.

1. The Victim's stance is, "There's nothing I can do!" Victims feel oppressed, helpless, hopeless, powerless, and ashamed, and seem unable to make decisions, solve problems, take pleasure in life, or achieve insight.

2. The Rescuer's line is, "Let me help you." A rescuer feels guilty if they don't go to the rescue. Yet their rescuing has negative effects: it keeps the Victim dependent and gives the Victim permission to fail. The Rescuer takes care of or takes over for others, often feeling fulfilled by this role but also exhausted and unacknowledged.

3. The Persecutor insists, "It's all your fault." The Persecutor is controlling, blaming, critical, oppressive, angry, authoritarian, rigid, and superior.

The model also includes a fourth role identified and added by Davies and Frawley (1994):

4. The Neglectful Bystander: This role represents individuals who remain uninvolved or are neglectful. It is similar to the role of

the persecutor but is more passive; it can represent, for example, a neglectful parent who turned a blind eye to abuse.

These roles are considered fluid and not fixed personality types. Individuals may shift between these roles, sometimes within the same interaction. The Karpman Triangle is often used in the analysis of conflict in individual or group therapy to help individuals recognize and stop participating in "drama cycles," ultimately aiming for more constructive interaction patterns.

Here's how these roles might apply to the trainee and client in the presented vignette:

» The client consciously or unconsciously enters the dynamic as the victim, harbouring a deep-rooted hope for care and attention that was absent in their upbringing.

» The therapist initially takes on the rescuer role by offering to bring the stuffing, possibly to mitigate the client's past pain, and perhaps unaware of the power they bring to bear in a mental health institution/relationship.

» By denying the impact of her promise to the client and forgetting the stuffing, the therapist inadvertently hurts the client and becomes the neglectful bystander, reminiscent of the client's neglectful caregivers and a confirmation that caregivers can harm.

» The disappointment and hurt felt by the client might cast the therapist into the perpetrator role, too. Despite her intentions and remorse, breaking a promise is experienced as a form of emotional harm and neglect.

In the vignette, the therapist trainee, perhaps unconsciously unaware of their need to be the saviour, steps into a role that resonates with the client's past—the promise of bringing stuffing symbolizes a potential relief from the client's history of neglect. However, the therapist's self-disclosure, the breaking of a promise and minimizing it as forgetfulness, may unconsciously repeat painful dynamics that the client experienced as a child, thus re-enacting the client's trauma and harming them.

Enactments occur when both the client and therapist are drawn into a pattern of interaction that replicates the client's historical relational dynamics. The client's request and the therapist's offer regarding the stuffing could be viewed as an enactment, wherein the therapist unintentionally adopts the role of a potential 'rescuer' or 'nourisher,' contrasting the neglectful figures from the client's past. However, when the therapist forgets the stuffing, this act, albeit accidental, shifts the dynamic, with the therapist now inadvertently occupying the role of a 'neglectful bystander,' a role familiar to the client from past experiences.

Attending to the unconscious process to prevent re-traumatization

In order to prevent harming the client by re-traumatization or effectively attending to the wounds of re-traumatization, the therapist needs first to be aware of their own emotional reactions to the story of the client, including the more intense ones. In the case presented, it would be the therapist's reactions to neglect and deprivation. The therapist can ask themselves, or use supervision to explore, these questions:

» How has the story affected me and informed my stance toward the client?

» How might this information lead me to deviate from the therapeutic frame?

» What will it mean if I gift this client something (in particular, items of food)?

» How does the client see me as a person in the world, and as a result, what fantasy might get projected onto me (i.e. explore the transference)?

Clark et al. (2015) suggest strategies to break free from these re-enactments by developing two-way empathy to help move beyond the perpetrator-victim roles, finding empowerment for the victim role, pausing and waiting instead of rescuing and becoming a mindful observer for the neglectful bystander role. Applied to the vignette, this strategy would mean:

> » Empathizing with the client's experience of disappointment, recognizing how the therapist's forgetfulness may have mirrored the client's past neglect.

> » The client could be encouraged to articulate their feelings of neglect, which may help them regain a sense of agency and move out of the victim role.

> » The therapist would benefit from pausing to understand her impulses to rescue, which may inadvertently disempower the client.

> » The therapist needs to acknowledge the harm and must become a mindful observer as a way to acknowledge the hurt in the re-enactment dynamics and consciously choose to engage with the client in a healing and present-oriented manner.

Some therapists will appreciate working within the original triangle in the therapeutic context while others may want to take this blueprint and work toward a change or skills-based treatment plan. In his book, David Emerald (2016) discusses The Empowerment Dynamic (TED), which is an alternative to the Drama Triangle, and aims to provide a guide for a more positive conceptualization. Transitioning to The Empowerment Dynamic would look like this:

Instead of being stuck in the Victim role, the client can be encouraged to become a Creator. This would involve the client expressing desires and needs directly and working on strategies to fulfil them, thereby taking ownership of her emotional well-being.

The therapist can transition from Rescuer to Coach. In this role, the therapist would support the client in discovering her own strengths and resources to meet her emotional needs. This could involve helping the client build a support system outside of therapy or fostering skills for the client to create her own meaningful traditions.

Rather than being seen as a Persecutor, the therapist can adopt the role of Challenger. The therapist can challenge the client to confront old patterns of thought and behavior that maintain the Victim stance and to practice new, healthier ways of relating to herself and others.

The Drama Triangle and The Empowerment Triangle are both useful. However, they should be used as theoretical frameworks and not a stencil. As a framework, we're still speculating about the unconscious process and its possibilities. As a rigid stencil, we can only see clinical and worldly relationships as exact replicas of the designated roles.

Anti-oppressive approaches to unconscious speculation

All clinical models and theories have limitations. However, many theories can also be re-read through an anti-oppressive lens without being rendered completely disposable. There are three main critiques and cautions when applying the concepts of repetition compulsion and unconscious role response.

1. Pathologizing Culturally Normative Behavior

Freud's concept of repetition compulsion can be seen as pathologizing survival strategies or culturally normative behaviors. For instance, individuals from marginalized communities may have to repeatedly navigate traumatic or oppressive systems, which is not necessarily a compulsion but a reality of systemic inequality.

Sandler's concept of unconscious role response could potentially overlook the structural and systemic factors that influence role-taking.

For example, power dynamics related to race, class, gender and other social identities can compel individuals to adopt certain roles for survival rather than due to unconscious processes alone.

2. Individualizing Systemic Issues

Both theories focus on individual psychology and intrapsychic processes, which can lead to the individualization of issues that are systemic and structural. This focus may inadvertently or intentionally place responsibility on individuals for their responses to oppression rather than acknowledging and addressing the broader societal factors that perpetuate inequality. This can be a form of victim blaming.

3. Over-emphasis on Unconscious Processes

The emphasis on unconscious processes can overshadow the conscious, rational strategies people from oppressed groups use to cope with and resist oppression. It may also understate the role of conscious agency and the capacity for individuals to intentionally change their responses to oppressive dynamics. It can rely on the idea of a white subject as the norm for health.

Conclusion

This paper underscores the critical importance of integrating an understanding of the impact that unconscious processes have on trauma-informed care in social work and psychotherapy. An exploration of psychoanalytic theories and concepts, such as Freud's repetition compulsion and Sandler's unconscious role responsiveness, coupled with practical examples and vignettes, illuminate how unconscious dynamics play a significant role in both client behavior and therapeutic interactions. The case studies presented, particularly the poignant vignette involving a forgotten Thanksgiving stuffing during therapy, serve as a powerful reminder of the complexities inherent in the therapeutic relationship, especially when navigating the delicate terrain of trauma.

By considering the unconscious elements of transference, countertransference, and enactments within the therapeutic setting, we can work toward a more nuanced and comprehensive approach to trauma-informed care. This approach emphasizes the need for therapists to be vigilant, hold themselves accountable, and be reflective about their own unconscious influences and the potential for re-traumatization and harming the client. Additionally, we can integrate an anti-oppressive lens, cautioning against the over-simplification of complex psychodynamic processes while maintaining a balanced view that acknowledges both individual psychological dynamics and broader systemic factors.

Ultimately, this paper advocates for a trauma-informed practice that is deeply attuned to the unconscious elements at play, fostering a therapeutic environment of safety, empathy and empowerment. This approach not only enriches the therapeutic process but also significantly contributes to the healing and recovery journey of those who have experienced trauma. By considering both the conscious and unconscious aspects of trauma, therapists and social workers can more effectively support their clients towards resilience, healing and a greater understanding of themselves and their experiences.

References

Akhtar, S., & O'Neil, M. K. (2011). *On Freud's Beyond The Pleasure Principle.* (1st ed.). Routledge.

Brown, V. B., Harris, M., & Fallot, R. (2013). Moving toward trauma-informed practice in addiction treatment: A collaborative model of agency assessment. *Journal of Psychoactive Drugs*, 45(5), 386–393.

Cherry, K. (2023, May 19). *What Is Repetition Compulsion?* Very Well Mind. https://www.verywellmind.com/what-is-repetition-compulsion-7253403

Clark, C. (2014). Transference and countertransference. In Clark, C., Classen, C. C., Fourt, A., & Shetty, M. (2014). *Treating the trauma survivor: an essential guide to trauma-informed care.* (pp. 119–129). Routledge.

Davies, J. M., & Frawley, M. G. (1994). *Treating The Adult Survivor Of Childhood Sexual Abuse*. Basic Books.

Elliott, D.E., Bjelajac, P., Fallot, R.D., Markoff, L.S. and Reed, B.G. (2005), Trauma-informed or trauma-denied: Principles and implementation of trauma-informed services for women. J. *Community Psychology*, 33: 461-477.

Emerald, D. (2016). *The power of TED : the empowerment dynamic*. Polaris Publishing.

Fallot, R. D., & Harris, M. (2005). Integrated trauma services teams for women survivors with alcohol and other drug problems and co-occurring mental disorders. *Alcoholism Treatment Quarterly*, 22(3-4), 181–199.

Frayn, D. H. (1996). Enactments: An evolving dyadic concept of acting out. *American Journal of Psychotherapy*, 50(2), 194–207.

Freud, A. (1936). *The Ego and the mechanisms of defence*. The Hogarth Press and the Institute of Psycho-Analysis.

Freud, S. (1918). From the History of an Infantile Neurosis. *The Standard Edition of the Complete Psychological Works of Sigmund Freud, Volume XVII (1917-1919): An Infantile Neurosis and Other Works*, 1-124

Freud, S. (1961). *Beyond the pleasure principle*. New York: Liveright Pub.Corp.

Harris, M., & Fallot, R. D. (2001a). Designing trauma-informed addictions services. *New Directions for Mental Health Services*, 2001(89), 57–73.

Harris, M., & Fallot, R. D. (2001b). Envisioning a trauma-informed service system: A vital paradigm shift. *New Directions for Mental Health Services*, 2001(89), 3–22.

Jung, C. G. (1968). *Man and His Symbols*. Dell.

Karpman, S. B., M.D. (2011). Fairy tales and script drama analysis. *Group Facilitation*, (11), 49-52.

Kernberg, O. F. (2005). The influence of Joseph Sandler's work on contemporary psycho-analysis. *Psychoanalytic Inquiry*, 25(2), 173–183.

Klein, M. (1946). Notes on some schizoid mechanisms. *The International Journal of Psycho-Analysis*, 27, 99-110.

Levenson, J. (2020). Translating trauma-informed principles into social work practice. *Social Work*, 65(3), 288–298.

Posadas, M. (2023). How do Psychoanalytic Mental Health Clinicians' Reactions, Understandings and Formulations Shape Their Work with Gender-Creative LGBTQ+ Clients? (Publication No. TBD) [Doctoral Dissertation, Smith College School for Social Work]. ProQuest Dissertations and Theses Database.

McWilliams, N. (2011). *Psychoanalytic diagnosis, second edition: Understanding personality structure in the clinical process*. Guilford Press.

Pain, C., Hunter, J., Ravitz, P., Maunder, R., & Leszcz, M. (2015). *Psychotherapy essentials to go: Achieving psychotherapy effectiveness*. W. W. Norton & Company.

Sandler, A.-M., & Sandler, J. (1998). Chapter Three: On role-responsiveness. In *Internal Objects Revisited* (pp. 47–56). Routledge.

Shedler, J. (2010). The efficacy of psychodynamic psychotherapy. *American Psychologist*, 65(2), 98-109. https://doi.org/10.1037/a0018378

The Narcissistic Abuse Industrial Complex: De-Centering Narcissism Within the Discourse on Relational Abuse and Trauma

TANYA GAUM, LMFT

In recent years, narcissism and 'narcissistic abuse' have increasingly become central themes and foci within the mainstream discourse on relational abuse and trauma, shifting the focus away from social, systemic, and structural issues that inform, enable, and perpetuate the cycles of intergenerational abuse and trauma, and raising concerns about how this discourse shapes our understanding of abusive dynamics. This chapter discusses the concerning outcomes of this growing focus on narcissism and 'narcissistic abuse' and challenges the ethics and efficacy of centering narcissism within educational resources for understanding and healing from the trauma of abusive relationships.

The term 'narcissistic abuse' was introduced in the mid-90s by psychologist Sam Vaknin; and has become an increasingly popular term for describing the constellation of manipulative behaviors that comprise emotional and psychological abuse such as *love-bombing, grooming, gaslighting, invalidation, stonewalling, isolation, coercion, rage, degradation, devaluation, blame-shifting, smear campaigning, and discarding.*

Conflating abuse with narcissism shifted the focus for understanding abusive behaviors away from social and systemic issues, as per classical domestic violence research, and more toward individuals and their individual pathologies. This provided survivors the validation they were seeking, especially those who were not physically assaulted by the abuser, because it gave them something more tangible to grasp onto to understand and *explain* their relationships that had become so confusing, chaotic, and in many cases, terrifying – Narcissistic Personality Disorder (NPD) and the less clinical label, 'narcissistic personality style.' By pathologizing the abuser and individualizing abusive behaviors, many survivors found it more possible to access relief from the painful and destabilizing self-blame, cognitive dissonance, and rumination caused by the abuse, most acutely by the gaslighting. These survivors began to identify as 'survivors of narcissistic abuse' and have steadily flocked to the teachings of Vaknin and other emerging specialists and educators on narcissism, NPD, and 'narcissistic abuse,' eventually growing into a movement.

The rapid growth of this 'narcissistic abuse' movement proved a great *demand* from suffering survivors that could easily be capitalized on by offering *supply* in the form of books, subscriptions, healing courses, social media platforms, podcasts, monetized YouTube videos, training for therapists, and therapy and life-coaching services specializing in 'narcissistic abuse.' What was once a well-intended movement for raising awareness and building a supportive community has morphed into what I refer to here as the Narcissistic Abuse Industrial Complex – an extremely lucrative, competitive, and often predatory web of therapists, psychiatrists, psychologists, life coaches, cult recovery specialists, spiritual healers, yoga instructors, advocates, activists, writers, social media influencers, family law attorneys, and divorce and custody mediators who have discovered that if they include 'narcissistic abuse' within their marketing materials, they are sure to succeed.

Centering narcissism within the discourse on relational abuse and trauma is problematic because it leads to a discourse that centers cis-hetero white survivors, placates oppressive dominant ideologies, and perpetuates the cycle of interpersonal and systemic abuse, oppression, and trauma. Centering narcissism individualizes abusive behaviors, thus *de-centering* and often excluding the trauma caused by systemic and structural oppression and further marginalizing survivors who are systemically, systematically, and structurally oppressed. In her chapter, *Attacks on Linking: The Unconscious Pull To Dissociate Individuals From Their Social Context*, Lynne Layton stated, "Dominant ideology works very diligently on a number of fronts to hide the systemic nature of inequalities of all kinds, to make sure that an individual's problems seem just that – individual" (Layton in Gutwill, p. 108). Layton's analysis of how dominant ideologies conceal systemic inequalities highlights a critical flaw in the 'narcissistic abuse' discourse. By framing abuse as an individual pathology, this discourse ignores the systemic roots of relational violence, reinforcing Layton's point that focusing on personal traits rather than societal structures perpetuates oppression. By centering narcissism within the discourse on relational abuse and trauma, the Narcissistic Abuse Industrial Complex seems to have become a red herring, distracting survivors from the root of relational abuse and trauma – *colonialism* – and its legacy of delusional hierarchies, oppressive inequities, and abusive dynamics within our relationships, families, communities, and institutions.

Colonized and colonizing systems create colonized and colonizing relationships

In his book, *Decolonizing Psychoanalytic Technique: Putting Freud on Fanon's Couch*, Daniel José Gaztambide (2024) discussed the concept of "colonial cannibalism" (p. 175) in the context of abusive dynamics. He referenced the works of Hungarian psychoanalyst, Sándor Ferenczi, stating:

> "In his Clinical Diary Ferenczi (1988) developed a theory of how abusers 'colonize' the mind of the abused to derive pleasure and soothe their own suffering, a psychic parasitic cannibalism. In an almost passing comment, Ferenczi extends this process beyond the intimacies of the family or interpersonal relations into 'hatred [of] a whole nation, a whole species' (p. 78). Ferenczi underscores how the environment's recognition of the self in spatial terms determines one's value—if I am not valued I feel 'small' and 'lesser,' dissolving to the point of 'death.' But if I can make the other feel small, I enlarge my value and position (Gaztambide, 2024, p. 181)."

Colonialism refers to the process where powerful nations have historically subjugated and exploited Indigenous populations, and continue to do so in some regions, leaving a dark legacy of systemic oppression. Systemic oppression refers to social, structural, and institutional practices that disadvantage, subjugate, and marginalize specific groups and individuals. These concepts are crucial to understanding how abusive dynamics are perpetuated beyond individual pathologies and personality styles. Gaztambide and Ferenczi's insights reveal how closely colonialism and the act of colonizing are related to relational abuse and trauma and how in many cases what survivors are enduring in abusive relationships is essentially the experience of being colonized by the abuser. True healing from relational abuse and trauma requires an understanding of the historical and systemic factors contributing to trauma and expanding beyond individual pathology; breaking the cycles of abuse requires breaking the oppressive systems that inform, enable, and maintain oppressive interpersonal dynamics.

Many therapists who specialize in 'narcissistic abuse' confidently claim to 'get it' in reference to the painful and confusing experience of being invalidated, gaslighted, and devalued by people we believed we could trust. Yet, without the cultural humility and trauma-informed lens that develops through being intentionally attuned to the traumatic and intergenerational impacts of colonialism and systemic oppression, many of these therapists don't truly 'get it' or even understand that they don't, which can lead to unintentional retraumatizing reenactments for their clients. For example: the therapist might invalidate their client by minimizing the significance of the client's ancestors' displacement or genocide due to settler colonialism, or they might *gaslight* their client by implying that the client doesn't 'get it' if the client chooses to focus less on the abuser's narcissism as the problem, and more on the abuser's classist, misogynistic, transphobic, or white supremacist beliefs and behaviors. Or the therapist might succumb to their own narcissism, displaying ego-fragility and defensive grandiosity, if the client attempts to confront them about their harmful inadvertent invalidations and gaslighting.

De-centering narcissism within the discourse on relational abuse and trauma doesn't negate the role that narcissism can play in abusive dynamics; it simply creates space for the marginalized discourse on colonialism and systemic oppression, which is essential for understanding and healing from abusive dynamics to reach the center of our purview. By shifting our focus to these broader systemic issues, we can develop more inclusive and trauma-informed strategies for addressing and healing from abuse, recognizing the diverse experiences of all survivors.

As Gwen Hunnicutt (2009) states in her article, *Varieties of patriarchy and violence against women: Resurrecting "patriarchy" as a theoretical tool*, "Without centering our focus on the social structures within which the victimization occurs, our treatment focus defaults toward the individual characteristics of the perpetrator and/or the victim. Consequently, individuals are often pathologized, and 'sick social arrangements'" (p. 556) are largely ignored. Hunnicutt's emphasis on the importance of analyzing social structures, such as patriarchy, in understanding violence against women parallels the need to de-center narcissism within the discourse on relational abuse and trauma. Her work supports the idea that without centering systemic factors, we risk individualizing abusive dynamics and ignoring the societal dynamics that sustain abuse. By centering the *root*, therapists, and others who hold space for survivors are better positioned to help survivors truly understand what happened to them, learn how to heal from the trauma, build a higher capacity for empathy, critical self-reflection, and accountability, and avoid causing harm to others and becoming 'the narcissist' in someone else's story.

Selective empathy and the problematic narcissist / empath binary

Despite generations of research and literature on narcissism, we still don't have a clear or collectively agreed-upon definition. From Sigmund Freud to the latest social media influencer on "narcissistic abuse," the discourse on narcissism has created more questions than answers regarding what narcissism, or a 'narcissist,' actually is, and why and how so many people become so harmful to others without remorse, accountability, consequence, or repair.

In his book, *Traumatic Narcissism: Relational Systems of Subjugation* (2014), narcissism and cult expert, Daniel Shaw, exemplifies the myriad complexities and contradictions embedded in the research and discourse on narcissism:

> Are we talking about 'healthy,' 'normal,' or 'pathological' narcissism? Is a narcissist deflated, overinflated, thick- or thin-skinned, overt or inverted? Is narcissism characterized by entitled grandiosity, or by primitive idealization, or both? Is it a line of development of the self, leading in maturity to empathy, wisdom, and humor; or a primitive infantile developmental stage to which schizophrenics regress? Is narcissism more broadly the dimension of mental activity concerned with maintenance of self-esteem? A pathology caused by an excessive endowment of aggression, or envy, or an extraordinary vulnerability to shame, or by traumatic impingements at crucial developmental stages? What about problems with making fluid transitions from subjective to objective states, and back—isn't that characteristic of the narcissist as well? All of the above is the answer, and a great deal more, when we go by the rich, complex, and sometimes contradictory psychoanalytic literature (p.1).

To assuage the confusion surrounding the definition and etiology of narcissism, and to relieve the burden of having to hold so much nuance, the Narcissistic Abuse Industrial Complex cherry-picks what can easily be packaged and sold from the extant literature on narcissism and discards the rest. Survivors are, thus, not being educated on actual narcissism but rather, they are being sold a constructed narrative that reduces narcissism to only a pejorative term, that frames *narcissistic* as the worst personality trait a person could ever have, that dehumanizes anyone arbitrarily labeled 'a narcissist,' and that promotes the concept of the narcissist/empath dichotomy, overtly conveying the message that certain people are inherently narcissistic and abusive while others are inherently non-narcissistic and non-abusive and that it is the survivor's high capacity for empathy and compassion that *attracts* the 'narcissist,' and consequently the abuse— *"If I was abused by a narcissist then, by default, I'm an empath, and I'm not narcissistic or abusive at all."*

What better way to attract and attach a massive population to a lucrative 'wellness' industry than to promote a narrative that convinces survivor consumers that their victimization evidences their inherent goodness and moral superiority? And what better way to perpetuate the cycle of relational abuse and trauma than to relieve survivors of the 'burden' of critical self-reflection, personal accountability, and civic responsibility by assuring them that they could never possibly victimize others?

Abuse is NEVER the fault of the victim. There is only *one* abuser and *one* victim in an abusive relationship. At the same time, while a person can be the victim in one relationship where they have *less* privilege, power, and protection in relation to the abuser, that same person can be the abuser in different relationships where they have *more* privilege, power, and protection. As myisha t. hill writes in her book, *Heal Your Way Forward: The Co-Conspirator's Guide To an Antiracist Future* (2022), "While we may have many unique experiences, we often play out our individual oppression in our interpersonal relationships" (p.30). For example – a white woman could be abused by her spouse or partner, and enduring the oppression of patriarchy in both private and public domains, AND she could be consistently gaslighting, invalidating, stonewalling, devaluing, and smearing her Black, Brown, and Indigenous colleagues at work.

Abuse is abuse. And genuinely empathetic people are not selective with their empathy.

Many survivors who hold the unearned privileges of being white, cisgender, and heterosexual don't seem to notice or consider the many problematic underpinnings of the Narcissistic Abuse Industrial Complex. For example – the specialists and educators on 'narcissistic abuse' publicly discuss political issues that directly impact cis-hetero white survivors such as patriarchy, gender-based violence, and corruption within the family court system, yet they claim to 'not want to get political' to try to justify their silence about abuses of power that directly impact marginalized survivors such as white supremacy culture, inequities toward people with disabilities, anti-trans legislations, and genocides against people who are Black, Brown, and Indigenous.

Many survivors also don't seem to notice or consider that all the books, articles, and YouTube videos on 'narcissistic abuse' that they consume and promote exclusively center and prioritize the needs, experiences, and comfort of white cis-hetero survivors – rarely even mentioning the existence of anyone else, or that these resources also center and prioritize the knowledge of white cis-hetero experts and educators, almost entirely dismissing the abundance of research, expertise, and experiential and ancestral knowledge from Black, Brown, and Indigenous scholars. An entire collection of works on interpersonal and systemic oppression, intergenerational trauma, epigenetics, and decolonized approaches to mental health and healing is excluded and dismissed by the writers and content creators who center narcissism and 'narcissistic abuse' within the discourse on relational abuse and trauma. If the tremendous contributions by Black, Brown, and Indigenous experts and educators are included at all in books about 'narcissistic abuse,' they are tokenized as a wise and compelling quote for an epigraph – never amplified, engaged with, or discussed within the body of the book.

It is important to note that there is a significant difference between a well-resourced therapist and a help-seeking survivor who might have limited awareness of the impact of their unearned privilege and is perhaps understandably too preoccupied with their personal emancipation and survival to engage with their empathy for others. It is also important to note that many survivors of abuse do happen to align with oppressive ideologies and even actively engage in abusive behaviors toward individuals and groups who they devalue or dehumanize. While some grace and benefit of the doubt can be extended to survivors in, or in the early wake of, an abusive relationship for seeming to not notice or consider entire demographics of survivors being excluded from the resources they find so helpful – I find it reckless to extend the same grace to therapists and other mental healthcare service providers who have the ethical responsibility to prioritize the needs of the most vulnerable populations, and to do the personal work of examining our harmful biases that could impede our ability and motivation to do so.

I understand that my tone might seem harsh and off-putting to some readers. Like many writers who critique oppressive dominant cultural norms, I had to choose between writing with a tone that is palatable for the more privileged, whose problematic practices I am scrutinizing, or a tone that is validating for the more marginalized whom I hope to affirm by saying, "Yes. I see you, and I see what you see." I chose the latter. In a recent post on X, A. R. Moxon wrote, "The most corrosive thing about civility discourse is that it presupposes that there exists some posture that marginalized people can take that would be submissive enough to preclude the violence their abusers intend, which implicitly blames them for the violence they experience" (2024). Rather than ascribing to victim-blaming palatability norms by centering white comfort, I chose to match my words with my behaviors (and tone) by prioritizing the comfort of systematically marginalized readers and joining their collective outrage with my own.

Renowned white experts on relational abuse and trauma versus the Narcissistic Abuse Industrial Complex

Like most mental healthcare spaces, the Narcissistic Abuse Industrial Complex is white-dominated, so limitations in terms of cultural experience and awareness are unavoidable. Being white, however, is not a valid justification for completely excluding systemic and structural oppression from the discourse and education on relational abuse and trauma, especially for therapists and other mental healthcare service providers who claim to be trauma-informed.

Lundy Bancroft—a cis-hetero white man—demonstrated back in 2002 a very clear understanding of systemic oppression, and how the abusive dynamics in our relationships, families, and communities are microcosms of the abusive dynamics in our systems. In his book, *Why does he do that?: Inside The Minds of Angry and Controlling Men*, Bancroft (2002) wrote:

> "If you look at any oppressive organization or system, from a racist country club up to a military government, you will find most of the same behaviors and justifications by the powerful... The tactics of control, the intimidation of victims who try to protest, the undermining of efforts at independence, the negative distortions about the victims in order to cast blame upon them, the careful cultivation of the public image of the oppressors—all are present, along with many other parallels. The people in power generally tell lies while simultaneously working hard to silence the voices of the people who are being dominated and to stop them from thinking, just as the abusive man strives to do. And the bottom line is the same: Oppressive systems stay in existence because the people in power enjoy the luxury of their position and become unwilling to give up the privileges they win through taking advantage of other people and keeping them down (p.331-332)."

Many other renowned white experts on relational abuse and trauma who do *not* center narcissism have also been acknowledging and addressing systemic and structural oppression, and de-centering white comfort within their respective books:

In *The Myth of Normal: Trauma, Illness, and Healing in a Toxic Culture*, co-written with Daniel Maté, Dr. Gabor Maté wrote, "Social attitudes, prejudices, and policies burden, stress, and exclude certain segments of the population, thereby increasing their propensity for suffering" (2022, p. 252).

In *Trauma and Recovery: The Aftermath of Violence—From Domestic Abuse To Political Terror*, Dr. Judith Herman wrote, "Only an ongoing connection with a global political movement for human rights could ultimately sustain our ability to speak about unspeakable things" (1992, p. 72).

In *Us: Getting Past You & Me to Build a More Loving Relationship*, Terrence Real wrote, "maintaining the system requires blunted empathy, dissociation, compartmentalization, and even faulty thinking" (2022, p. 275).

In *What Happened to You?: Conversations on Trauma, Resilience, and Healing*, co-written with Oprah Winfrey, Dr. Bruce Perry wrote, "The privileged groups turn their gaze from the pain. In the face of systemic racism, we say, 'Look how far they've come'; in the face of cultural genocide, 'They need to assimilate'; in the face of trauma, 'Isn't it great that they are resilient.' It is so easy to create an 'other'" (2021, pp. 187-188), and he also stated, "I believe that if you don't recognize the built-in biases in yourself and the structural biases in your systems—biases regarding race, gender, sexual orientation—you can't truly be trauma-informed" (2021, p.220).

The call from these trauma-informed authors to acknowledge and address systemic oppression, and for a connection with global human rights movements to sustain discourse on trauma, underscores the necessity of integrating systemic considerations. This aligns with the chapter's critique of the narcissism-centered approach, advocating for a broader understanding that includes systemic oppression within all resources and spaces that engage with the discourse on relational abuse and trauma. Such discussions about systemic oppression, human rights, our built-in biases and *othering* of people, and our collective enabling of oppressive systems are nowhere to be found in the books, articles, healing courses, social media content, or YouTube videos about 'narcissistic abuse.' How can survivors truly understand, heal from, and break the cycles of relational abuse and trauma without receiving comprehensive education about the oppressive systems and structures that create and enable abusive dynamics, and contribute to their pervasiveness?

In an attempt to evidence this concerning pedagogical gap within the Narcissistic Abuse Industrial Complex, in a way that readers could cross-check on their own, I conducted a word search on Kindle in ten of the most popular and best-selling books on 'narcissistic abuse.' The search showed how many times terms related to abuse, trauma, and systemic oppression were found in each book. The results for the total number of times selected terms (and all variations of each term) found within the 10 books were as follows: narcissism = 5613; abuse = 1426; gaslight = 702; invalidation = 116; superiority = 87; trauma = 875; violence = 49; compassion = 202; empathy = 425; healing = 1039; supremacy = 0; systemic oppression = 0; oppression = 3; colonize = 0; decolonize = 1; marginalize = 1; discrimination = 1; racism = 6; homophobia or transphobia = 0; BIPOC or POGM = 0; LGBTQ = 2; ableism = 0; disability = 1; classism = 0; white fragility = 0; patriarchy = 1; equity = 0; intersectionality = 0; microaggressions = 0; subjugation = 0; somatic = 3.

I also pulled a few concerning and dehumanizing quotes, that seem to nod toward eugenics, from popular social media platforms. I will paraphrase here to avoid singling anyone out: "Narcissists should be isolated together on a deserted island;" "People with Cluster B personality disorders should never have or have access to children;"

"Narcissists are not amenable to clinical treatment;" "Narcissists never change;" "Narcissists are evil monsters."

The *mainstream* discourse on narcissism and 'narcissistic abuse' has essentially become a gentrification of the more marginalized discourse on colonialism and systemic oppression to make the discourse on abuse and trauma more palatable for the most profitable consumers— white cis-hetero survivors who, in many cases, prefer to recover from abusive relationships without feeling 'burdened' by having to consider their own narcissism or the ways that survivors of abuse can *also* be abusive and oppressive, even if inadvertently.

The Narcissistic Abuse Industrial Complex could even be considered a *grift* through its exploitation of survivors who are desperately seeking relief from the pain of empathy-deprived relationships while simultaneously enabling the survivor's own low or selective empathy. The grift exploits this empathy deficit in the way that 'narcissistic abuse' specialists encourage survivors to conceptualize their loved ones who don't support or validate them enough as 'narcissist enablers,' and even to go no-contact with these loved ones, further isolating already-isolated survivors and further attaching them to the often monetized content and offerings of the Narcissistic Abuse Industrial Complex. For example: a survivor could call her sister in an emotionally dysregulated state with the hope of immediate comfort, validation, and support. If the sister responds with any amount of frustration, overwhelm, or shortness, the survivor has been indoctrinated by the Narcissistic Abuse Industrial Complex to interpret this response as unempathetic and therefore narcissistic. It doesn't matter that the sister might have been making dinner, helping her child with homework, arguing with her own husband, and unprepared to hold space in an attuned manner or that the survivor didn't engage her empathy by checking in with her sister first to determine of it was a good time to talk; the significant relationship is now ruptured and the survivor is further relegated to the 'narcissistic abuse' support groups and healing programs to access support and receive unconditional validation that her sister is a 'narcissist' or a 'narcissist enabler.'

Critical self-reflection versus the delusion of supremacy

As previously mentioned, educators on 'narcissistic abuse' endorse a narcissist/empath binary, teaching survivors that people are either narcissistic or non-narcissistic, abusive or non-abusive, and that 'narcissists' are attracted to 'empaths,' or highly empathetic people. This dichotomy has led many confused survivors, who *know* they have their own interpersonal flaws and limitations (as all humans do), to ask themselves, and their therapists: "What if *I'm* the narcissist?" The educators on 'narcissistic abuse' answer: "Even asking that question proves you're not the narcissist because narcissistic people don't critically self-reflect...*you* are a good and compassionate *empath*; *they* are the evil and abusive *narcissist*." A simple internet search with entries such as "narcissist, empath" or "Am I the narcissist?" will produce thousands of articles, books, and social media posts that substantiate my observations and concerns.

Through a more trauma-informed, classical domestic violence lens – abusive relationships are not a symptom of individual pathologies, but rather a symptom of oppressive colonized systems that inform, encourage, and enable oppressive interpersonal biases, beliefs, and inequities. Bancroft (2002) substantiated this argument, writing "abusiveness has little to do with psychological problems and everything to do with values and beliefs" (p. 319) and "[the abuser's] value system is unhealthy, not their psychology" (p.38). The most fertile ground for an abusive dynamic to develop is a relationship where there is an imbalance of privilege, power, and social protection that many people are socialized to believe they are entitled to exploit. "Wherever power imbalances exist, such as between men and women, or adults and children, or between rich and poor, some people will take advantage of those circumstances for their own purposes" (Bancroft, 2002, p. 123).

As I write this chapter, the world has been witnessing a live-streamed genocide of Palestinians for exactly a year and the U.S. is mere weeks away from the most divisive and complex presidential election the country has ever endured. I have seen countless posts on social media labeling Israeli Prime Minister Netanyahu and former U.S. President Donald Trump a "narcissist," a "psychopath," a "monster." Despite whatever psychological make-up or personality style Netanyahu might have, his sense of entitlement to perpetrate such unimaginable violence is clearly bolstered by social and political systems that have been built to uphold, maintain, and protect colonialist, imperialist, capitalist, and white supremacist interests. The impulse to pathologize and dehumanize both Netanyahu and Trump as a way to explain their behaviors is rooted in our desire to distance ourselves from the violence and destruction they continue to cause and call for; to see ourselves as apart from it, not complicit in any way in also upholding, maintaining, and protecting the oppressive systems that created them and continue to enable their harms and destructiveness.

In his article, *I Helped Write The Manual For Diagnosing Mental Illness. Donald Trump Doesn't Meet The Criteria,* Allen Frances (2017) framed the popular impulse to diagnose the former president with NPD or to label him a "narcissist" as a distraction from the harmful behaviors that he has been enabled by the systems to perpetrate. Frances warned his readers, writing, "I believe that Trump is a mirror of the American soul, a surface symptom of our deeper societal disease...We mustn't waste this Trumpian dark age. If we don't learn from it, we will keep making the same mistakes (para 14)." I will add that if we don't also learn from our collective enabling response to the extreme violence, oppression, and genocide perpetrated against Palestinians, we won't learn how to confront and heal our own collective narcissism toward collective liberation.

Narcissism is certainly helpful for understanding the motives and modus operandi of some abusive individuals, but by using *only* the lens of narcissism to discuss and explain relational abuse and trauma, educators on 'narcissistic abuse' are ignoring, denying, and minimizing the root of the problem that encourages, enables, and empowers certain individuals to gratify their narcissistic desires— colonialism, and the invasive weeds of systemic oppression and supremacy culture that have spread from that root.

A person's narcissism, if heightened, might cause them to want to be granted more comfort, consideration, convenience, and control than others, but it is cis-hetero ableist patriarchal white supremacy culture that deludes many people into believing that they are entitled to protection from accountability for whatever harm they might inflict upon others in their efforts to access all that comfort, consideration, convenience, and control. This is why some people are more abusive and destructive than others, regardless of their respective levels of narcissism.

Individualizing abusive behaviors and pathologizing individuals who behave abusively also creates the illusion that relational abuse and trauma can be avoided by identifying and receding from abusive individuals, or 'narcissists,' which ignores and invalidates the realities for systematically marginalized and oppressed people who have no escape or liberation from the abuse because the system can also be the perpetrator and enabler of their abuse. The categorical abusive/non-abusive binary allows survivors who prefer to avoid critical self-reflection and personal accountability regarding how they enable and benefit from the system to set themselves apart from all the violence and harm in this world, and to protect their social and self-image as only and always *empathetic, compassionate*, and *good*.

Sonya Renee Taylor, author of *The Body Is Not an Apology: The Power of Radical Self-Love*, discussed in a podcast interview about her book how "white supremacist delusion" (Taylor & Doyle, 2023) shapes harmful social hierarchies, making us vulnerable to harmful relationships with ourselves and others. Her insights align with this chapter's argument that systemic oppression must be central to our understanding of relational dynamics, and provide a crucial perspective for understanding relational abuse and trauma beyond individual narcissism. Taylor explained, "as long as there are people below us, then we know we're better than something even if that's not conscious, at least I'm not down there…And so the fear is whatever I got at rung eight, I'm going to drop to rung three. If I denounce the ways in which white supremacist delusion has indoctrinated me, then I'm going to lose the perks that whiteness gives me. And I don't want to acknowledge all the perks that whiteness gives me because then that makes me a bad person." (Taylor & Doyle, 2023).

Renowned psychoanalyst and culture critic Dr. Erich Fromm spoke to this delusion of supremacy in the context of our normative individual and group narcissism which he described as, "ceasing to have an authentic interest in the outside world but instead an intense attachment to oneself, to one's own group, clan, religion, nation, race, etc.-with consequent serious distortions of rational judgment" (1965, p.99). In his 1963 lecture titled Nationalism As An Expression of Group Narcissism, Fromm explained,

> "the normal and neurotic narcissism in all of us implies one thing, that we are not fully open to the world, that we are more or less, filled with our own ego and, therefore, that there is something like a veil between ourselves and the world and it is simply a matter of degree how thick that veil is. How immovable it is. How often it is torn or raised."

Fromm's analysis of group narcissism as a veil obstructing authentic engagement with the world reinforces the need to address systemic issues. By linking Fromm's ideas to the current discussion, we see how focusing solely on individual narcissism can perpetuate broader social delusions of supremacy.

Lifting the veil, the delusion of supremacy, and acknowledging the world around us requires a high capacity for empathy for others, as well as for ourselves. When empathy is discussed within the Narcissistic Abuse Industrial Complex, however, it is within the context of the survivor's exploited empathy for the abuser – never, or very rarely, in the context of the survivor's empathy for themselves, or for the other people the abuser might be harming: the abuser's family members; their exes they call 'crazy;' the children they share with their exes; their restaurant server or Uber driver; their employees; their colleagues; their clients; or, in many cases, those who are harmed by their commitment to racist, homophobic, transphobic, fatphobic, misogynistic, ableist, or classist beliefs and behaviors.

The Narcissistic Abuse Industrial Complex doesn't encourage survivors to scrutinize or recede from people who are racist, homophobic, transphobic, fatphobic, misogynistic, ableist, or classist. The 'narcissistic abuse' specialists tell people to avoid, leave, and go no-contact with 'narcissists,' yet they never include these oppressive forms of bigotry in their descriptions of a 'narcissist,' or deem them harmful enough to warrant ending a relationship.

The Narcissistic Abuse Industrial Complex and traumatic reenactments

In their article, Whiteness As Pathological Narcissism, Arianne E. Miller and Lawrence Josephs wrote, "To confront someone about one's repudiated white privilege is analogous to confronting the person about their defensive grandiosity; the person feels attacked and responds with denial and counterattack" (2009, p. 93). When a person holds white privilege, "the advantages of being white, whether acknowledged or not" (2009, p. 93), or the ultimate unearned privilege— "White-Patriarchal-Christian Privilege, which is a particular kind of narcissism" (Shaw, 2022, p. 92) —their capacity for critical self-reflection is compromised. When a person's white privilege is coupled with a strong attachment to being perceived as highly *empathetic, compassionate,* and *good* (as to not be perceived as "a narcissist"), their defensive grandiosity can reach even greater magnitudes, causing them to become an incredibly difficult person to confront about even the slightest grievance, thus causing others to walk on eggshells.

In her article, "Post-Traumatic Slave Syndrome Revisited," Dr. Heather Hall wrote:

> There is still the possibility that one might feel guilty about the harm done to the other. This guilt needs silencing as well. To do so, the most malevolent perpetrators insist that the victim admit that they deserve the abuse. In these cases, the victim realizes that the only way to minimize the pain's intensity is to help the perpetrator assuage the guilt by saying that yes, I did deserve it. That is the final soul-crushing blow to the victim. The scars left by this are profound, long-lasting, and challenging to overcome (2021, para 7).

Most survivors of relational abuse and trauma understand all too well this self-negating survival strategy. They remember the many times they placated the abuser's delusion of supremacy, apologized to them for 'causing' their cruelty, and offered the abuser the 'reflection of perfection' they needed to alleviate their guilt and shame. Many spaces where survivors gather within the Narcissistic Abuse Industrial Complex create retraumatizing reenactments of this abusive dynamic, often inadvertently, through their unquestioned and perhaps unconscious, demand that marginalized survivors center the feelings of the most privileged and powerful in the group, while censoring their own.

Because the 'narcissistic abuse experts' tend to minimize, dismiss, invalidate, and exclude the experiences, needs, knowledge, and trauma of people who are Black, Brown, Indigenous, queer, trans, fat, and disabled, many vulnerable marginalized survivors who are lured into the Narcissistic Abuse Industrial Complex are tasked with having to gaslight themselves into believing they matter to these 'experts' and to 'go along to get along' – to fawn and perform 'agreement' to their own subjugation as to not trigger the discomfort of guilt and shame for the more privileged and powerful members of the 'community' that subjugates them. They have to silently say "Yes, I did deserve it" (Hall, 2021, para 7) – the invalidation and exclusion – in order to access whatever support they can to help reduce the pain, confusion, fear, and isolation of the abusive relationships and systems they are navigating or trying to recover from.

Herman stated, "The more powerful the perpetrator, the greater is his prerogative to name and define reality, and the more completely his arguments prevail (1992, p. 15)." Fromm also stated, "The narcissistic fiction is confirmed by consensus of our reality (1963)." Perhaps it is time for both survivors and survivor-serving professionals to stop gaslighting ourselves into believing the 'experts' and educators on 'narcissistic abuse' are all *good* and *empathetic* and *well-meaning*, and to start reflecting back to them the reality of *the outside world* that they have been enabled by far too many people to ignore...and invalidate.

References

Bancroft, L. (2003). *Why does he do that?: Inside the minds of angry and controlling men.* Penguin.

Doyle, G., & Wombach, A. (Hosts). (2023, January 12). Sonya Renee Taylor: What If You

Loved Your Body? (No. 168) [Audio podcast transcript]. In *You Can Do Hard Things.* https://momastery.com/blog/we-can-do-hard-things-ep-168

Frances, A. I helped write the manual for diagnosing mental illness. Donald Trump doesn't meet the criteria." *STAT News*, September 6, 2017, https://www.statnews.com/2017/09/06/donald-trump-mental-illness-diagnosis/

Fromm, E. (1964). *The heart of man: Its genius for good and evil.* Harper & Row, New York.

Fromm, E. (1965). Credo. In E. Fromm, (1994). *On Being Human.* New York, pp. 99-105. https://fromm-online.org/en/life/erich-fromms-credo/

Gaztambide, D. J. (2024). *Decolonizing psychoanalytic technique: Putting freud on fanon's couch.* Palgrave Macmillan.

Layton, L., Hollander, N. C., & Gutwill, S. (Eds.). (2006). *Psychoanalysis, class and politics: Encounters in the clinical setting.* Routledge.

Hall, H. "Trauma and dissociation in the news: Post-traumatic slavery syndrome revisited." *International Society for the Study of Trauma and Dissociation (ISSTD) News*, January 22, 2021, https://news.isst-d.org/post-traumatic-slavery-syndrome-revisited/.

hill, m.t. (2022). *Heal your way forward: The co-conspirator's guide to an antiracist future.* Row House.

Herman, J. L. (1992). *Trauma and recovery: The aftermath of violence—from domestic abuse to political terror.* Basic Books.

Hannicutt, G. (2009). Varieties of patriarchy and violence against women: Resurrecting "Patriarchy as a theoretical tool." *Violence Against Women*, 15(5), 553-573.

Maté, G., and Maté, D. (2022). *The myth of normal: Trauma, illness, and healing in a toxic culture.* Avery.

Miller, A. E., & Josephs, L. (2009). Whiteness as pathological narcissism. *Contemporary Psychoanalysis, 45*(1), 93–119. https://doi.org/10.1080/00107530.2009.10745989

Mullan, Moxon, A. R. (2024). X post, July 14.

Real, T. (2022). *Us: Getting Past You & Me to Build a More Loving Relationship.* Rodale Books.

Shaw, D. (2014). *Traumatic narcissism: Relational systems of subjugation.* Routledge.

Shaw, D. (2022). *Traumatic narcissism and recovery: Leaving the prison of shame and fear.* Taylor & Francis.

The 92nd Street Y, New York. (April 18, 1963). Nationalism as an Expression of Narcissism, with Erich Fromm. [Audio]. https://www.youtube.com/watch?v=ckRgGgdjzBs

Winfrey, O., Perry, B. D. (2021). *What happened to you?: Conversations on trauma, resilience, and healing.* Flatiron Books.

About the Contributors

Carm De Santis, MSc, RP, RCFT

Carm De Santis, MSc, RP, RCFT, is an assistant professor (teaching stream) in the Department of Sexualities, Relationships, and Families (SRF) - formerly the Department of Sexuality, Marriage, and Family Studies (SMF) at St. Jerome's University in the University of Waterloo with a private relational and sex therapy and supervision practice. She facilitates courses that focus on the principles and practices of systemic thinking, social justice, inclusivity, and anti-oppression. Carm aims to support learners in conceptualizing and applying these practices into meaningful and therapeutic interventions while attending to intersecting identities in diverse contexts. She is constantly exploring innovative ways to weave theory and research into her practice as an educator, researcher, relational and sex therapist, and supervisor. Carm is invigorated by my interactions and conversations with students, clinical supervisees, and colleagues that tackle questions about justice, accessibility, and diversity, and that interrogate colonialism, white supremacy, and patriarchy. Her passion for lifelong learning and inter-disciplinary training affords her the opportunity to work collaboratively with researchers and clinicians from various disciplines (e.g., sexology, family studies, social psychology, social work, counselling, medicine).

Carm's research and clinical interests traverse sexual and relational well-being over the lifespan; diversity, inclusivity, and social justice; experiential learning; and self-reflection and transformational learning. Her doctoral dissertation focuses on consensual non-monogamy, inclusionary practices, and the constructs of pleasure.

Tanya Gaum, LMFT

Tanya Gaum, M.Ed., M.A., LMFT, specializes in healing and recovery from relational abuse and trauma. She approaches her therapeutic work through a womanist, decolonizing, LGBTQIA+ affirming lens, drawing primarily from Humanistic Therapy, Narrative Therapy, and Family Systems Therapy models, as well as psychoanalytic, deconstructionist, and queer theoretical frameworks. One of her greatest joys is witnessing a person's eyes begin to open to how much strength, courage, and resilience they actually have to exist in this world as who they truly are. Tanya is queer, Canadian, and Jewish. Her Los Angeles-based private practice offers therapy, coaching, and professional consultation services.

Pratyusha Tummala-Narra, Ph.D.

Dr. Tummala-Narra is a Professor of Counseling, Developmental, and Educational Psychology at Boston College. Her research and scholarship focus on immigration, trauma, and culturally informed psychoanalytic psychotherapy. She is also a clinical psychologist in Independent Practice and works primarily with survivors of trauma from diverse sociocultural backgrounds. Dr. Tummala-Narra is an Associate Editor of Psychoanalytic Dialogues and the Asian American Journal of Psychology. She is a member of the Holmes Commission on Racial Equality in American Psychoanalysis, initiated by the American

Psychoanalytic Association, and a member of the Board of Directors of the Psychotherapy Action Network (PsiAN). She is the author of *Psychoanalytic Theory and Cultural Competence in Psychotherapy* (2016), the editor of *Trauma and Racial Minority Immigrants: Turmoil, Uncertainty, and Resistance* (2021), and co-author of *Applying Multiculturalism: An Ecological Approach to the Multicultural Guidelines* (2023), all published by the American Psychological Association Books.

Marco Posadas, PhD, RSW

Dr. Posadas is a psychoanalyst member of the International Psychoanalytical Association (IPA), Clinical Social Worker, Licensed Psychologist (MEX), and earned his PhD at Smith College School for Social Work in Northampton, Massachusetts. He currently operates a clinical practice in Psychotherapy, Psychoanalysis, Clinical Supervision and Consultation in Toronto, Canada. Dr. Posadas is a member of the Canadian Psychoanalytic Society, the Mexican Psychoanalytic Association, and he is the 2024-205 Antoinette Calabria visiting scholar for the Psychoanalytic Center of the Carolinas.

He is the inaugural Chair of the Gender and Sexual Diversity Studies Committee of the IPA, where he developed the IPA's sexual and gender diversity strategic plan, and the creation of the first IPA Tiresias award. He received the Sue Fairbanks Excellence in Psychoanalytic Knowledge Distinguished Lecturer award at the University of Texas at Austin - Steve Hicks School of Social Work in 2018. Dr. Posadas served on the Board of Directors of the Ontario Association of Social Workers (OASW) where he was recipient of the 2013 OASW Inspirational Leader Award for his work with underserved and marginalized populations, and the Distinguished Social Worker for Toronto award in 2022.

Rahim Thawer, MSW, RSW

Rahim Thawer (he/him) contributed to this volume from his perspective as a clinical social worker and psychotherapist. He also edited the volume. Read his full bio in the "About the Editor" section.

About the Editor

Rahim Thawer (he/him) is a registered social worker (OCSWSSW), Certified Clinical Supervisor (CCS), and psychotherapist originally from Treaty 13 territory, which encompasses the land of present-day Toronto—derived from the Mohawk word *tkaronto*, meaning "where there are trees standing in the water." He is a faculty member in the School of Social Work at The University of Alabama, where he is completing a Doctor of Social Work (DSW) with a specialization in organizational leadership.

Rahim has taught as an adjunct lecturer at two colleges and three universities across Ontario and serves as an ongoing course facilitator in the University of British Columbia's *Certificate in Equity, Diversity, and Inclusion* program. He also teaches *Foundations of Sex Therapy* annually as part of Wilfred Laurier University's Continuing Education program. His clinical, teaching, and research work sit at the intersection of mental health, social justice, and psychoanalysis, exploring how anti-racist and queer-affirming frameworks can support social workers, therapists-in-training, and organizational leaders.

Rahim hosted a video podcast series called *The CBT Dive* (2020-2023) to demonstrate the use of cognitive behavioral therapy tools with the goal of demystifying clinical work and building reference material for therapist trainees. To support this mission, he has also developed and self-published reference guides on therapy assessment, clinical documentation, and making sense of common countertransference responses in the therapeutic space.

Rahim has dedicated over a decade of volunteer service to LGBTQ Muslim community organizing and currently maintains the international *Queer & Trans Muslim Speakers' (QTMS) Directory*, advancing his mission to amplify community voices and intersectional perspectives. He also founded the Canadian Queer & Trans Therapists (CQTT) Directory, a subscription-based platform that enhances culturally competent and timely access to affirming mental health care across the country.

Since starting his private psychotherapy and consulting practice in 2014, Rahim has delivered over 200 presentations across Canada and internationally. His workshops and consultations foster critical dialogue on systemic oppression, sexual health, clinical interventions, and innovation in queer relationships. He explores many of these topics online and at thepoliticizedpractitioner.com.

He is the co-editor of *Any Other Way: How Toronto Got Queer* (Coach House Books, 2017), a finalist for the Toronto Book Awards, and the author of *The Mental Health Guide for Cis and Trans Queer Guys* (New Harbinger Publications, 2025). His forthcoming titles include *Queer & Muslim: On Faith, Family, and Healing* (Co-Editor, University of Regina Press, 2026) and *Sexualized Substance Use: A Guide for Mental Health Professionals* (Taylor & Francis, 2028).

Honours and Awards

Leadership & Professional Awards

» *Humanitarian Award* — American Association for Sexuality Educators, Counselors and Therapists (AASECT, 2025)

» *Mary Smith Arnold Anti-Oppression Award* — Counselors for Social Justice (CSJ), American Counseling Association (2025)

» *Toronto-Area Distinguished Leader Award* — Ontario Association of Social Workers (OASW, 2024)

Academic & Scholarly Distinction

» *Research Fellowship* — Saint Louis Psychoanalytic Institute (2025/2026)

» *Faculty Fellows Program* — University of Alabama Gen-Ed Digital Literacy Initiative (Fall 2025)

» *Gina Ogden Curatorial Scholarship for Integrative Approaches to Sex Research and Therapy* — Kinsey Institute, Indiana University (2025)

» *DSW Award for Writing to Advance Social Work and Social Justice* — The University of Alabama (2025)

Community & Cultural Recognition

» *Honorary Award in Education* — South Asian Americans for Change (SAAFC, 2025)

» *Champion Award* — 25 Champions/25 Years, Alliance for South Asian AIDS Prevention (ASAAP, 2020)

» *Proud to Shine Toronto Community Award* — Canadian Broadcasting Corporation (CBC, 2018)

About the Press

Blue Cactus Press is an independent publisher. Our mission is to craft books and experiences that spark dialogue about liberation. Our books are written and crafted by people from historically marginalized groups. We believe books can be used as tools for dreaming new worlds and realities into existence, and for bridging the gap between words and action.

We envision a world in which books empower & celebrate communities we walk in. We strive to implement equitable business models that center collective liberation as the rule, not the exception, and offer makers dignity, autonomy, and creative voice in our practices. We work toward a future in which our planet is prioritized over profit and publishing practices are accessible and gate-free.

We seek creatively satisfying, financially viable, and relationally resonant work. We value curiosity, craftsmanship, and relational responsibility among humans, our environment, and other living organisms.

To support the press, please request our books at libraries, become a member at patreon.com/bluecactuspress or purchase our books at bluecactuspress.com.

Practice & Politics: The Essential Reader For Social Workers And Therapists.
Volume 1, The Politicized Practitioner Series
Edited by Rahim Thawer, MSW, RSW

ISBN: 978-1-967633-00-5
First edition.

Permissions:

Bathhouse Counselling, Or the Relevance of Psychoanalytic Interventions In Clinical Social Work by Marco Posadas, PhD, RSW. Reprinted with permission. Published online: 25 May 2018. PSYCHOANALYTIC SOCIAL WORK. 2018, VOL. 25, NO. 1, 56–73. https://doi.org/10.1080/15228878.2018.1472022

Portions of the land acknowledgement used in this book, particularly text written in the Twulshootseed language, are from the Puyallup Tribal Language Program website. The mission of this program is, "to be kind, be helpful and be sharing in terms of revitalizing the Twulshootseed language by producing language users." We thank the Puyallup Tribal Language Program for the use of this valuable resource. Find out more about the Puyallup Tribal Language Program at puyalluptriballanguage.org.

Blue Cactus Press | caləɫali

www.ingramcontent.com/pod-product-compliance
Lightning Source LLC
Chambersburg PA
CBHW052020030426
42335CB00026B/3226